THE NATIONAL WRITERS ASSOCIATION GUIDE TO WRITING FOR BEGINNERS

A How-To Reference for Plot, Dialogue, Nonfiction, Internet Publishing, and More

Sandy Whelchel

Rowman & Littlefield Education
Lanham, Maryland • Toronto • Plymouth, UK
2008

Published in the United States of America
by Rowman & Littlefield Education
A Division of Rowman & Littlefield Publishers, Inc.
A wholly owned subsidiary of The Rowman & Littlefield Publishing Group, Inc.
4501 Forbes Boulevard, Suite 200, Lanham, Maryland 20706
www.rowmaneducation.com

Estover Road
Plymouth PL6 7PY
United Kingdom

British Library Cataloguing in Publication Information Available

Library of Congress Cataloging-in-Publication Data

Whelchel, Sandy.
  The National Writers Association guide to writing for beginners : a how-to
reference for plot, dialogue, nonfiction, internet publishing, and more / Sandy
Whelchel.
     p. cm.
  Includes index.
  ISBN-13: 978-1-57886-685-4 (hardcover : alk. paper)
  ISBN-10: 1-57886-685-5 (hardcover : alk. paper)
  1. Authorship. 2. Authorship—Marketing. I. National Writers Association
(U.S.). II. Title.

  PN147.W447 2008
  808'.02—dc22
                                                        2007027301

♾™ The paper used in this publication meets the minimum requirements of
American National Standard for Information Sciences—Permanence of Paper
for Printed Library Materials, ANSI/NISO Z39.48-1992.
Manufactured in the United States of America.

CONTENTS

INTRODUCTION

For the past 25 years, I have taught beginning and advanced writing classes—first in my home, later in parks and recreation departments, at a local community college, and finally as executive director of the National Writers Association. In that period of time, I have read countless books on beginning writing, how to write, and the esoteric process of writing. From each text, I gleaned a certain kernel of truth but also by-passed thousands of useless words. Some books concentrated on the process, some concentrated on the essence, but few gave the basics. Each book left me feeling frustrated and unwilling to recommend them to my students because they lacked some of the essentials or assumed that the student knew more than he or she did.

Writing this book has evolved from the urging of my countless students who suggested that if I didn't like anything currently on the market, I should write my own. I shrank from this task because I felt there were already too many "how to write" books out there. But this task is now coming to fruition through the encouragement of my friends—my students—my loyal fan club who really believes I have something to offer others on the process of writing. I glow with pride at their accomplishments, which include everything from publication in the local newspaper and winning first place in the National Writers Association

Novel Contest to the ultimate book contract and agent representation. This book is for them and for every person who shares the dream of someday getting published.

For the reader's benefit, the chapters are short in order to provide opportunity to utilize the information on his or her own project.

❶

GETTING STARTED

You want to write. You've said it a million times. You've told your friends and family that you are finally going to get started on that book/article/short story/poetry that you've always said you were going to write. Now what?

A PLACE TO BE

As elementary as it may sound, the first thing you need is a place to write. This place can not be the kitchen counter, the dining room table, or a folding table in the corner of your bedroom. It must be a place where you can be alone with your thoughts, ideas, and writing—away from the television, radio, screaming kids, or telephone, and preferably as far from the refrigerator as possible. Whether it is a converted closet, a corner of the basement, or, as mine is, a converted room that once served as the nursery, it needs to be totally *yours*.

It should be a place where your writing can be left out in the open— without invading troops from the toddler crowd or the hungry teenage hordes. It should be a corner where you can be as messy or tidy as you prefer. Translation: Your writing place should have a door so you can shut out the prying eyes of visitors, neighbors, or your mother-in-law. It is, as my daughter used to say, "my room and I need it."

This room is hallowed ground. Visitors are admitted only with your permission. Families with a bit of training can learn to enter only in cases of dire emergencies, for example, the house burning down.

STOCKING YOUR WORKPLACE

Now that you have your workplace, what do you need to get started? I started with the basics and built as money permitted. The basics include pens, pencils, a stack of yellow pads, a good dictionary, a copy of *Elements of Style* by William Strunk Jr. and E. B. White (4th ed., Needleham Heights, MA: Allyn and Bacon, 1999), and a typewriter or computer. As finances permitted I added a thesaurus, a good encyclopedia (eventually on CD-ROM), an instant reference guide, a dictionary of quotations, *The Chicago Manual of Style* (15th ed., Chicago: University of Chicago Press, 2003), and, ultimately, a computer. With the current low cost of computers, I personally suggest using a computer. The amount of paper used in typing and retyping works will pay for a computer in less than 1 year for even the most part-time, beginning writer on earth. A computer with Microsoft Word will eliminate a thesaurus, encyclopedias, and a dictionary, so you'll save money there, too. Manuscripts must be typed, so the would-be writer must at least have a typewriter. Typewritten work with the inevitable errors will not garner as much respect from an editor as will a computer-generated piece. If you are using a typewriter, you may be getting rejections that have nothing to do with the merit of the piece and more to do with the messy typewritten text.

Today more and more editors and writers insist you need a computer before you begin writing. If it is financially feasible at all, I suggest moving into the 21st century with a computer. I am aware that many people are not comfortable using a computer, but it truly is not that difficult. On a personal note, I am sure I have saved an entire forest by using a computer instead of the old typewriter, but a computer may fall into the luxury—not necessity—category.

The last two basics are not found in any store, and only you can provide them. The first is *desire*. I cannot enumerate the times I have had someone tell me they have always wanted to write. The statement falls second only to the weather in frequency of topics of discussion with strangers who learn I am an author. You must want to be a writer and want to tell your story more than sleeping or eating. You must have the desire to get your thoughts and ideas on paper or your efforts will fail. Meeting with friends for lunch or the urge to go shopping can't supersede your desire to write.

The second necessity is *tenacity* or *perseverance*. Sticking through 20 pages of a story or article or 250 pages of a novel or nonfiction book takes tenacity. Sticking through 200 rejection slips on that story or book takes even more tenacity. Living with family or friends who question your interest in writing or even scoff at your writing accomplishments takes perseverance, but if you have the dream—the fire in your belly—you can succeed. So let's go!

WRITE REGULARLY

We all know people who are going to write that novel, family history piece, or poem—*someday*. The difference between a successful writer and a "wannabe" lies in a regular commitment to his or her craft. Write every day or at least on the same schedule you'd keep on a regular job. Because most writers must maintain another job, they learn to write in irregular blocks of time or at irregular hours. Some rise early in the morning and work until they must go to another job. Others write during evenings and weekends to accomplish a project, but they all *write*.

For the purpose of beginning, try to pick a time in every day to dedicate to a few minutes of work. This means putting down the remote control for the television and the joystick for video games. It means working on your writing during specific times. Once you get into the habit of doing this, choosing to do other tasks will begin to make you feel guilty about not using that time for your writing. Yes, we know you have a family and other commitments. There will be times when taking children to soccer practice takes precedence over writing, but even when waiting for the carpool, a piece of yellow paper can record ideas you can save for later.

Some writers I know work through weeks at a time when they're working on a regular project. Others take off weekends or a month during the

☞ **EXERCISE**

Take a few moments to write down why you want to write. This doesn't need to be more than a few sentences. It will help you focus when you get stuck or discouraged. Post it on a bulletin board near your writing place.

summer. Because mailing manuscripts is not advised during busy postal seasons, some writers take off the time from Thanksgiving through January 1. I have found that this period of time is one of my most productive and, although I don't mail out manuscripts during this time, I work to finish pieces to mail after the first of the year.

Find a schedule that works best for you. The most important thing is to write and keep writing on some sort of a regular basis.

SUMMARY

All writers need a place away from interruptions to work. The place to work should be stocked with writing tools (writing instruments, a dictionary, and, ultimately, a computer, although many writers still use yellow legal tablets and pencils). The two most important tools for a writer are desire and tenacity. To be successful, a writer must write on a regular schedule.

❷

IDEAS, IDEAS, IDEAS

Authors will tell you that the most frequent question they receive from workshop participants (after "What have you written?") is "Where do you get your ideas?" For the purpose of this book, it would seem logical that we could assume that you have an idea, or you wouldn't be reading a book on how to write. However, this is not always the case. Because I have had students who came to my class because (1) their astrologer told them they might have some talent for writing or (2) in the case of my friend Gary (a writer of some talent), the class was cheaper than a psychiatrist, we must concede that some people may need assistance in the *ideas* department.

WHERE TO GET IDEAS

1. Newspapers, magazines, and other books
2. Movies, television, or other visual media
3. Watching people in the mall, department stores, supermarket, or any other large meeting place
4. Good old-fashioned daydreaming
5. Conversations overheard in restaurants or anywhere
6. Your own life

> ☞ **EXERCISE**
>
> Clip six magazine or newspaper articles for use later. This is the beginning of
> your idea file. Keep them handy in a file folder at your desk.

Look around in your world; there are millions of possibilities for ideas;
you only have to look.

Now that you have enough ideas for several lifetimes—how are you
going to save them all?

STORING IDEAS

For most writers storing ideas tends to be a more difficult process than
getting them. Some of the best ideas tend to come at very inconvenient
times—on the freeway, at 3:00 a.m. in bed, in important business meetings, while you are on the cell phone, during an intimate kiss, and so on.
In some cases you might just lose the idea. (I suggest that during intimate kisses you do not rush for your paper and pencil. The same is true
for the freeway.) Yes, I, too, have seen those folks talking on the telephone, combing their hair, reading their mail, or, indeed, reading a
novel while driving down the freeway, but please for your own safety's
sake, do *not* read or attempt to write while rushing down the interstate.
Try to hold the idea until the next exit or when you've reached the safety
of your office or home.

Some of the best ways to keep ideas include journals, notebooks, and
notecards. *Journals* have long been used to store fragments of ideas for
writers. These fragments could include plot ideas, character possibilities, snatches of conversations, or phrases or words that will eventually
fit into something you write. Your journal can be as simple or as complex as you wish. Some authors use spiral notebooks. Others indulge in
blank-paged books from the local stationery store. Some use laptops or
Palm Pilots, Blackberries, or other new technologies. Whatever your
preference, it is your journal and you should use it in any way you find
appropriate. *Notebooks* can be carried in pockets and purses, and left on

the nightstand for those genius phrases that materialize at 3:00 a.m. Always carry a notebook, and keep those pieces of life in it that can be used to draw plots, characters, or valuable scenes. *Notecards* are as useful as notebook pages and have the added advantage of your being able to categorize them by characters, plots, dialogue, or scenes into a file card system for easier use in the future. Whatever system you decide will work for you, keep at it, don't quit doing it, and begin to build your writing elements file for your future projects. Add clippings of newspaper and magazine ideas and other information to supplement your writing ideas.

Someone who read this chapter questioned the use of tape recorders for recording ideas, suggesting that it was much safer when driving the freeway. I do not recommend tape recorders because they tend to lead to negative writing habits. People taping their material begin to think that their words are so wonderful, their voice so magical, that they refuse to edit and make a better piece of work. If you are a person who works well with recording, go ahead. But keep in mind that the recorded words, like written ones, must be honed and edited to garner a quality piece of work.

SUMMARY

Ideas for written pieces can come from other printed material, visual media, people watching, daydreaming, conversations, your own life, or the world around you. Stockpiling ideas can be difficult. Start a file folder or begin a journal; use a notebook, or begin to file on notecards. The most important thing to remember about ideas is they need to be saved. Tape recorders can be used if you remember to edit your spoken words.

③

WHERE ARE YOU GOING?

Now that you have ideas, you are ready for the next step. Where are you going? Which writing road will you take? What fork in that road will you choose? What are you going to write?

All writing falls into one of four categories: poetry, which I will not cover here because it is a different type of writing; nonfiction, or the presentation of facts and factual information into an article, essay, or nonfiction book; and fiction, the creation of imagination into believable, interesting short stories or novels.

Most fiction techniques are applicable to nonfiction. Both require a consistent storyline presented along with interesting people in a plausible, enjoyable manner. Each requires a hook to draw the reader in, as well as pacing, emotion, and development of reader interest to keep the piece moving.

LITERARY VERSUS MAINSTREAM

In the course of teaching creative writing, the question about literary writing versus mainstream is usually on the minds of at least several students. The line between the two disciplines is murky at best, but I will attempt to give the creative-writing student some idea of the differences.

☞ **EXERCISE**

Take a few moments to jot down several story ideas you think you would like to work on in the next few weeks. Store them in your idea file.

Literary writing tends to be more narrative and plot driven than mainstream writing. The pace of literary writing tends to be slower, and more description is used by literary writers. Personally, I enjoy reading an occasional "literary" novel, but if you are interested in eventually selling your work to a major publisher, I recommend sticking with mainstream writing.

Mainstream writing is more character and dialogue driven. The pace is faster, and there is more action taking place in a mainstream novel or short story. Description tends to be used in mainstream work to give the reader a flavor of where the action is taking place rather than being an integral part of the storyline.

Several genres are encompassed in the term *mainstream* in addition to what is called a regular mainstream novel. Genres in mainstream include romance, mystery, westerns, action/adventure, science fiction, horror, and thrillers. Several of these genres have subgenres. For instance, the romance field includes contemporary romance, romantic suspense, gothic, historical romances, and several small subcategories. Each genre includes a subgenre or two within its confines.

As an aside, if you are considering writing a romance novel, it is currently the most popular writing field. According to a *Publisher's Weekly* survey, 48% of all fiction books purchased were romances. Other genres pull somewhere from 7% to 14% of the market share of fiction books.

SUMMARY

Now that you have decided to write, you must make a decision about the type of material you want to write: poetry, fiction, or nonfiction. You may also wish to choose a subcategory or genre to write within. Literary work is more plot and narrative driven. Mainstream is more character and dialogue driven.

④

PROPER MANUSCRIPT FORMAT

One of the greatest faults with manuscripts from beginning writers lies in their nonconformity to proper manuscript format. Editors can spot a novice in seconds, and this automatically takes away more than 50% of your chances for publication. *Learn proper manuscript format!* It is not some nebulous thing that is secretly given only to professional writers. It is explained in the latest edition of *Writer's Market* and alluded to in almost every writing book.

SHORT STORIES AND ARTICLES

Proper manuscript format for short stories and articles is as follows: The first page includes your name, address, telephone number, and e-mail address and a line that reads "Social security number upon request" in the upper left-hand corner. The approximate word count and rights you are selling should be typed in the upper right-hand corner. It is inadvisable to place a copyright symbol on any work sent for publication. Most editors know the penalties for copyright infringement and are offended to have anyone indicate they might plagiarize.

The actual text begins 20 lines, or approximately 3 inches, down the page if you are using Microsoft Word, with the title and "by" with your name below it, centered and double spaced. Beginning halfway down the page gives the editor a place to make notes regarding headlines, type font, or any illustrations on the white space you have left for him or her.

The second and subsequent pages should include a header with your last name in the upper left corner, a brief form of the title centered, and page number at the upper right. Double space and begin your text. Another way to include this information is to place it in the right corner as follows: name/title/page number.

The manuscript should be double spaced, with 25 lines per page and 1-inch margins on all sides. With some computers, you will need to leave 1½-inch margins at the bottom in order to achieve 25 lines per page. If this formula is followed, it is easy for the editor to determine the length of the piece as it relates to the length needed for his or her space requirements. If your computer doesn't have that capability, you can also safely estimate that you have 250 words per page to calculate the approximate word length.

Never justify the right margin. In many word processing programs, this means literally going into the program and telling the program to unjustify the right margin. True, your manuscript will look nicer if the right side is justified, but this means that the space between words is changed and may again foul up an editor's estimate of the amount of space needed for a certain article.

Many computers offer orphan and widow protection as well as the option for italics or changing fonts. The orphans option changes the number of lines per page and once again fouls up the word count. Italics looks great and is currently accepted by most publishers to indicate thoughts.

Remember, being clever or cute is not going to impress an editor and may irritate him or her instead. You are preparing a product for sale to a specific audience. Editors, and eventually their readers, are the consumers. Putting red ribbons on a screwdriver is not going to sell the screwdriver any faster. Give the consumer (the editor) what he or she wants. The editor is the most critical reader you will ever have. Giving him or her what he or she wants will sell your work much faster.

BOOK MANUSCRIPTS

The format for the first page of a book-length work varies slightly from articles and short stories. Your name, address, telephone number, e-mail address, and "Social security number upon request" go in the upper left-hand corner of a cover page. Across from your name, show the approximate word count. Many authors feel the need to put a copyright notice on the second line. Once again, this is to be discouraged for several reasons: First, if your manuscript doesn't sell in the first year, the copyright notice instantly dates the work. Second, many editors feel the copyright notice is a sign of an amateur writer and will treat the manuscript in that manner.

Again, the author should space down 20 lines and center the title of the work (some agents and editors suggest the type of work be centered under the title, e.g., "A Romance Novel" or "A Western Novel"), then center the word *by*, insert two spaces down, and type in your name. If you are using a pseudonym, the pseudonym should be centered under *by* and the word *pseudonym* centered under the pseudonym. Because you have used your name in the upper corner, the editor is aware the book is being written under a pseudonym.

See Appendixes B and C for examples of proper format for first pages.

☞ EXERCISE

Take a few moments to familiarize yourself with proper manuscript format. This should become an important part of your writing. Using the correct format will ensure a closer look by every editor.

SPELLING AND GRAMMAR

Thinking about spelling and grammar can be like peeling potatoes. It is a dull, drudge job, but you have to do it before you get mashed potatoes or a presentable manuscript. Despite the prevailing belief by some writers, it is *not* the editor's job to correct spelling and grammar. Most modern computers have a spell-checker—*use it*—but keep in mind that the checker does not pick up the differences between *so* and *sew* or any other correctly spelled words presented in the wrong context. Thoroughly proofread your work. There are several recent "spelling dictionaries" currently on the market that can be added to your computer hard drive to complement your spell-checker. If spelling is your downfall, invest in one. Remember that it's quite simple to learn that the manila folder only rhymes with and is not spelled like *vanilla*. Your mistake may provide the editor with a chuckle but certainly won't ensure a sale. So for goodness sake, use the dictionary or spell-checker.

If you have problems with punctuation and grammar, invest in *The Chicago Manual of Style*. This handy guide gives examples of usage and punctuation. There are also several smaller, less expensive books, such as *Nitty-Gritty Grammar: A Not-So-Serious Guide to Clear Communication*, that cover most of the frequently committed grammar mistakes.

PROOFREADING AND CRITIQUING

No matter how hard we try or how knowledgeable we are of the new grammar rules, most writers fail to find their own mistakes. Proofread your work carefully. Then contact a friend, relative, writing colleague, or professional to proofread for grammar and spelling. The cleaner the manuscript, the more likely it is that an editor will be interested.

CRITIQUE GROUPS

Critique groups are discussed further in Chapter 18. For the sake of information at this point, every writer should consider attending a critique group.

Critique groups can be a thing of beauty or your worst nightmare. My current critique group falls close to the "thing of beauty" mark. Everyone is helpful and encouraging. One member goes as far as to preface her remarks by saying, "in my opinion." No one can give you exact information on a critique group, but here are some guidelines to determine if a particular critique group is right for you:

1. Groups of more than 10 tend to be too cumbersome and don't allow enough time for a thorough critique of each member's work.
2. Someone should act as a facilitator. The facilitator makes sure everyone has a chance to read and give his or her input.
3. Before joining a group, visit a couple of times and see if you are comfortable with the group dynamics.
4. It is recommended that group members give two positive comments for every negative one.
5. Part of the function of a critique group is to encourage each other. If one member fails to bring work for several meetings, encourage him or her to bring something.
6. Limit the number of pages of work to 15, maximum of 20. Anything longer means someone else loses out.
7. Spend a few minutes at the beginning or the end of the group exchanging marketing information and tips or plain old chitchat. Helpful information is dispensed at this time, too.
8. Recruit a "grammar maven." Someone who knows the rules of grammar is a valuable asset to the group.
9. A plethora of online critique groups are available. Drop in on a few before you decide if this is right for you. See if you can learn about the qualifications of some of the members. There is nothing more devastating than to receive an ego-smashing critique that leaves you feeling like plumbing should be your only endeavor only to learn later that the critique was penned by a 17-year-old who is getting Ds in English.

SUMMARY

Learning proper manuscript format will give you a better chance at selling your work. See Appendixes B and C of this book for the format of

first pages. Putting a copyright notice on the manuscript is not a suggested practice. It is not necessarily the job of the editor to correct
spelling and grammar. You, the writer, should be aware of spelling and
grammar errors and correct them.

WORK CITED

Fine, E. H., & Josephson, J. P. (1998). *Nitty-gritty grammar: A not-so-serious guide to clear communication.* Berkley, CA: Ten Speed Press.

5

GREAT BEGINNINGS

You have 5 seconds to catch an editor's eye. The editor is the most discerning reader you will ever have. And if you do not approach your story's beginning correctly, the editor may be the *only* reader you ever have. Crafting a great beginning is the most difficult task for a writer. Some writers write the entire story or article before they write the *hook* or *lead*. For others, hooks or leads seem natural and are the first thing to hit the paper. In this chapter, I explain the differences and similarities between these enigmas and assist the writer in crafting some hooks and leads.

THE FOUR-WAY SENTENCE

An easy beginning for your writing can be the four-way sentence. This can assist in shaking loose "writer's block" to get you into the writing mode. Some four-ways will work for a great beginning, but some do not and will end up being scrapped after the writer is more involved in the work.

The four-way sentence consists of the name of the central character, a descriptive phrase, a suggestion of where he or she is, and details on what he or she is doing. *Example*: Clancy's steel gray eyes scanned the dance floor. (The reader now knows the name of the central character, something about him, where he is, and what he is doing.) To most readers Clancy's last name is not germane and should be left out. Calling him Clancy Jones is unnecessary and may mark you as a beginner.

Perhaps one of my outstanding memories for a compelling opening hook sentence that is also a four-way sentence came from one of my beginning students who wrote, "The man who tried to rape me came back to knock on my door two nights later." One student shuddered; one sat with mouth agape; I'm sure my pupils dilated. She had us hooked. We all wanted to hear the rest of the story, and we weren't disappointed. You may have difficulty writing that gripping a beginning initially, but with practice you can succeed, and at the very least, a four-way sentence will get you into the meat of your story.

Any mechanism that assists you in getting into the writing mode is not only useful but necessary. If you have other ideas for beginnings, hold the four-way sentence for one of those rocky days when nothing seems to be going right.

THE HOOK

All writing needs a hook. If your four-way sentence won't pull your reader into the story, delete it and find the beginning most likely to lure that editor into your piece. In this section the words *hook* and *lead* will be used interchangeably. For purposes of understanding for the novice, *lead* is the term used by most writers and editors in the nonfiction field. *Hook* is the term used by most fiction writers. The purpose of both is the same—to entice your reader into the story so he or she does not want to quit reading. A hook does just that—it hooks the reader and keeps him or her on the line to the end. In short fiction or nonfiction, the hook must appear in the first sentence. Remember the "five-second rule"? That's all the time you have.

In book-length works, the hook or lead must appear in the first two pages and for best effect should occur in the first few sentences. Hooks or leads require readers to find an answer, thus making them read on to the conclusion. You must give the reader a reason to begin reading your material and, more importantly, a reason to read to the end.

Contemporary author Clive Cussler is a master of the hook. In his book *Cyclops*, he begins the first paragraph with the sentence "The Cyclops had less than one hour to live." The reader is immediately struck with questions: Why? What is going to happen? How can this be? And the reader is *hooked*. He or she will read on to find the answers to these questions. Cussler retains his title as master of the hook at the end of his introduction by ending the chapter with "She kept on going, down, down, until her shattered hull and the people it imprisoned fell against the restless sands of the sea floor below, leaving only a flight of bewildered seagulls to mark her fateful passage." Will the reader finish the book? Probably. Only the most jaded could put this power aside and not be haunted by the fateful passing of the Cyclops.

Remember the book that you kept on reading long after you pleaded exhaustion and swore you were going to bed? No doubt the chapter hooks kept you reading. Chapter hooks are a polished professional's device to keep you interested in the story and reading. Leads accomplish the same purpose in an article. In one of my own articles about a haunted house, I used a lead almost guaranteed to keep the reader reading: "Pots and pans fly from cupboards, and wallpaper rips with gunshot-like sounds." Yes, it is a hook. Yes, it is a fiction technique. Yes, it does work.

In a more straightforward article, the lead promises answers to come: "Jim Smith has found new growth on his balding head of 10 years." Every balding man wants to know what Jim is doing, and the article promises to tell them the secret. This straightforward *lead* gets the reader into the article with a promise of the panacea for balding men.

☞ EXERCISE

Use the four-way sentence to begin a story. Remember, you may not choose to use the sentence in your final draft, but this will assist you in getting started.

SELECTED READING

For examples of four-way sentences, I recommend the following:

- John Irving's *A Prayer for Owen Meany* (New York: William Morrow, 1989)
- Jack London's "War" in Grant Overton's *World's Fifty Best Short Novels*, Vol. 4 (pp. 126–133, New York: Funk and Wagnalls, 1929)

For hooks, I recommend the following readings:

- Clive Cussler's *Cyclops* (New York: Simon and Schuster, 1986), both the beginning sentence and final paragraph of the prologue
- Gary Paulsen's *Hatchet* (New York: Puffin Books, 1987) (outstanding chapter hook on page 12)

SUMMARY

You have five seconds to catch an editor's eye. This means you must hook your editor immediately. Good beginnings or hooks can be written with a four-way sentence that includes the name of the character, where he is, what he is doing, and one characteristic. If the four-way sentence will not work, you may need to write most of the work to find a *hook* that will keep your reader interested.

6

PLOTS AND STORYLINES

When you have your opening statement—your hook, your lead, your promise of things to come—you are ready to craft your story or article. Now the ugly word *plot* raises its head. Is this story going somewhere? Before you begin writing, while you are writing, and for sure before you get to the end, you need to know where your story is going. You need to know the plot.

Plot, simply put, is the shortened version of what your story is about. My writing mentor, Pat Stadley, once told me that you should be able to put the plot of your story on a matchbook cover. Not much room, but then the basic plot shouldn't take much room. The plot of *Moby Dick* is the struggle of one man against a whale. The plot of Hemingway's *Old Man and the Sea* is the story of an old fisherman's fight to land a massive fish.

Several techniques for plotting include constructing an outline, writing down notes, or at least developing an idea of the story's plot in your head. It seems like a simple enough concept, but many of the short stories entered in the National Writers Association Short Story Contest have *no* plot. Characters wander from one incident to another, and nothing holds them together. Or sometimes they wander to the very end and have no tie-in to the beginning, much less the middle, of the story.

Basic plotlines fall into one of several general categories:

1. Man against man. Classic examples: every mystery and Thomas Harris's *Red Dragon* and *Silence of the Lambs*.
2. Man against nature. Classic examples: Jack London's "To Build a Fire" or Ernest Hemingway's *Old Man and the Sea*.
3. Man against himself. Classic example: Charles Dickens's *A Christmas Carol*.

All short stories or novels fall into one of these general areas with perhaps a little overflow into one of the others.

METHODS OF PLOTTING

Outlining

Some writers can't begin writing until they have the total idea of the entire story or novel firmly fixed on paper. They sit down and write out an old-fashioned Roman numeral outline or a one-page narrative on what the story is about. Try these methods if you like. They don't work well for me, but many methodical writers feel either way is a must.

Synopsis

Many writers write the synopses of their novel before they begin. A synopsis is merely a one- to three-page narrative of what the story is about. Tell the story as you would tell a friend what you are writing.

In Your Mind

I prefer to have the basics in my head. They swim around there and have given me more than one sleepless night, but the plot is always there—unfolding and twisting to the whim of my characters.

Plot, therefore, is not a huge or complex problem. Plot is simply what the story is about. Storyline, on the other hand, can be the nemesis of the new writer.

STORYLINE

Storyline is the way the writer builds to the ultimate conclusion. Story-line is taking the initial hook or four-way sentence, building it into a scene, continuing to dramatize the scene, leading that scene into a series of rising dramatic scenes, each one connected with time or circumstance transitions. These scenes utilize flashbacks to give necessary information or retell less-important episodes until they reach a dramatic climax. Then the story or novel ends with a bang and as little end material as necessary.

IMPORTANT INFORMATION TO REMEMBER FOR YOUR STORYLINE

1. Never add a scene that is not necessary to the story.
2. Never use dialogue, narration, or a description that isn't important to the story.
3. Everything in the story should lead to the ultimate conclusion of the story.
4. *If it isn't important to the story, leave it out.*

These simple rules may sound a bit structured and unyielding, but if followed they will assist you in staying on track while you write. They will keep you from being pulled into a dead-end alley or off on a meaningless tangent.

Some writers need to have an outline of the story before they can begin. Others need to know exactly where the story is going before they can start writing. Still others insist on knowing the entire story right down to the ending sentence. Each of these is a matter of personality and style; no way is exactly the "right" way. You may have to experiment with several methods before you find the right one for you. I personally have a general idea of where a story is going before I begin. Sometimes I know the ultimate conclusion, but I find outlining hinders the full development of my characters, whom I try not to limit.

OTHER THOUGHTS

My newspaper/magazine training tends to force me in the direction of full-circle plots and storylines. That is, in some way the end of the story must relate directly to the beginning. If for no other reason than to force a *good* plot, this is a simple but effective way to make certain you do have a plot.

All memorable stories do not have to have an upbeat resolution. *Romeo and Juliet* is a good story. The resolution is obviously not a happy one. Your story does not necessarily have to have a twist. Most of the O'Henry stories have a twist, and for many years stories with a twist were the only stories accepted by magazines. Fortunately for all of us, this is no longer the case, although many fine "twist" stories are still written. Short stories by their nature do not allow too many twists or convolutions in plot and storyline. To try and place too much in less than 20 pages is not only difficult but leaves your reader confused or dissatisfied. *Never leave your reader confused or dissatisfied. If you do, your reader will leave you.*

ARTICLES AND NONFICTION BOOKS

We have spent a great deal of time discussing plots and storylines for fiction, but what about an article or nonfiction book? As stated earlier, an article should begin with the hook or lead. The bulk of the center material in the article should deal with proving the lead or hook. How did Mr. Smith begin to grow new hair? What causes the pots and pans to fly from the cupboards? What are scientists' theories on the increasingly cold air masses hitting the West Coast? The bulk of your article is dedicated to proving your lead, with the final paragraphs reiterating your original thesis.

For nonfiction books the idea is much the same. The core of the book is used to advance theories of the author, back up original statements with research ("facts and figures"), or elaborate on the original premise. Final chapters draw conclusions and reinforce the original material presented.

☞ **EXERCISE**

Analyze several short stories to find the basic plotline in each. Determine which type of plotline you feel comfortable with and consider slanting your writing in this direction. It is likely that the plotline you choose will be comfortable for you for further writing.

NEWSPAPER STYLE OF WRITING

Of course, somewhere in the back of the room, someone with a newspaper background is screaming. Most newspaper stories follow an entirely different sequence and look much like an inverted triangle. The hard facts of the story are contained in the first paragraph, with less important information contained in the subsequent paragraphs. Why? Because old newspaper editors cut from the bottom up. Therefore the most important information is where it won't be cut from the story. Many newspaper readers don't take time to read an entire article all the way to the end, so they want all the important stuff in the beginning of the article.

SELECTED READINGS

Most writers plot well. For outstanding plotting I recommend these authors: Mary Higgins Clark, Patricia Cornwell, Joseph Wambaugh, and Connie Willis.

SUMMARY

Plot is the basic direction your story will take. Three basic plotlines are man against man, man against himself, and man against nature. Plotting methods can include outlining, writing a synopsis, or simply forming the idea in your mind. Storyline is the series of scenes that take the reader to the ultimate conclusion of the story. Stories that go full circle are usually the most satisfactory for the reader. Articles and nonfiction books don't necessarily have a plot, but they do follow a format that brings the reader to some conclusion.

7

CHARACTERIZATION

The essence of all fiction writing falls into the realm of characters. Characters lead the action, give the work life, and make the reader interested in finding out more. Good characters give a story meaning and depth. Poor characters force the death knell of even the most outstanding plot.

Appendixes G and H are two examples of character development sheets. Feel free to use them at liberty; I have found them invaluable in getting to know my characters. "But I don't need to know that much information about my main character," you say. "Good grief, I could write the novel in the time it takes to fill out the sheet." You need to know everything about your characters, right down to what they ate for breakfast. This is not important—it is essential. Did they have granola at breakfast? It makes them a different person from the guy who had frosted flakes.

Even the minor character sheets are important. You may not find it disconcerting that your minor character's name on page 40 is Joe when it was Clem on page 5, but your readers will. They will also be upset that the raven-haired beauty on page 10 is a carrottop on page 92. Authors need credibility. The author who misses the details loses his credibility in a hurry.

More than one student has sighed in exasperation, "But where can I find characters?" Look around. My favorite places to find potential characters are shopping malls and grocery stores. Have you ever noted the different shoppers? There are the purposeful, determined confident shopper; the ambling, misdirected, unconcerned shopper; or the flighty, honeybee shopper flitting here and there. All have a different personality, a varied set of goals, and a perfect set of character traits for your work.

At this point it is wise to caution against stereotypes. Fat, dumb sheriffs, dingy blondes, and Brad Pitt handsome heroes are overused and tiresome. Create your own set of believable and interesting characters and then place them in a setting made for the voracious reader.

Much has been written recently about archetypes. In fact, entire books have been written about male and female archetypes. While this may work for some writers, I believe it detracts from making characters "real." The movie *Legally Blonde* is an example of how much fun can be found from adding human elements to the archetypes by inserting the determined and actually intelligent characteristic into the "dumb blonde."

Giving your characters flaws adds more dimension to them. Even Superman has a problem with Kryptonite. In *Open Season* and *Savage Run*, author C. J. Box's continuing character, Joe Pickett, is a game warden who can't shoot straight. Your readers don't want to see a perfect character. Readers have a problem identifying with perfect people because they know nobody's perfect. The flaws make more believable, sympathetic characters.

Frequently I am asked about drawing characters from my own life. Yes, every writer does it. A word of caution, however: Do it carefully. Some time ago, a letter crossed my desk guaranteed to send chills through any writer drawing characters from friends and relatives. Apparently an author had drawn too close a parallel between her best friend and a character in her writing. The subject of the letter was a potential libel and slander suit against the author.

Potential characters are everywhere. Pull up a chair and observe the world. You will find some of the most exciting and interesting characters are as close as your nearest community gathering.

KNOWING YOUR CHARACTERS

To emphasize again, in fiction you must know your characters. Without "missing a beat," you need to know how your character will react in any

---

☞ **EXERCISE**

Observe some people in public places and then use these observations to fill in your character sheets. Develop your story to include in your character some of the characteristics you've listed on the worksheet.

---

given situation. Will he or she run, freeze, or fight? Kiss and tell? Laugh or cry? When your character is presented with an untenable situation, you should be able to keep on writing because you know how your character will respond.

Generally, men should not try to write from a female viewpoint and vice versa. Most beginning writers have difficulty slipping into the viewpoint of the opposite sex. If you aren't able to "think like a man," your reader will know it and fail to believe your entire work. There's truth to the statement that "men are from Mars, women are from Venus." Writing from the opposite viewpoint is a difficult assignment. Some writers will argue that the best-selling novel *Memoirs of a Geisha* was written by a man, but even that finely crafted work had little subtleties that gave the author away.

SELECTED READINGS

For unforgettable characters, I recommend the following books or authors:

- C. J. Box's *Open Season* (New York: Putnam, 2001) and *Savage Run* (New York: Putnam, 2002)
- Richard Brautigan's *The Abortion* (New York: Simon and Schuster, 1971) and *The Hawkline Monster* (New York: Simon and Schuster, 1974)
- Thomas Harris's *Red Dragon* (New York: Delta Trade Paperbacks, 2005) and *Silence of the Lambs* (New York: St. Martin's Press, 1988)
- John Irving's *A Prayer for Owen Meany* (New York: Modern Library, 2002)
- Lawrence Sanders's *The Third Deadly Sin* (Boston: G. K. Hall, 1982)

SUMMARY

Characters are the essence of every piece of fiction. To draw unforget-table characters, the writer should know more about the characters than what will be used in the book. Avoid stereotypes and archetypes. Try to give your characters the "human" quality. Writing from the viewpoint of the opposite sex is difficult and not recommended for beginners. Good characters can be found in observing people around you and then draw-ing composites. If you draw characters from people in your own life, you must be careful about invasion-of-privacy complications.

⑧

DIALOGUE

Now that you have drawn and placed some of the most exciting characters into your writing, give them something to say! Idle chitchat that doesn't move the story forward is a waste of your reader's time and your effort. Dialogue should move the story forward or give the reader a better understanding of the character.

How? If necessary, it's back to the shopping mall. Other wonderful sources of conversation are hidden in your local restaurant or at the nearest party. Dig past the small talk about recipes and children; head for the heart of the conversation and what is really meant. Take out the *ands, uhs,* and *uh-uhs.* Condense the essence of the conversation. Now you have good dialogue. How would the main character hold this conversation? What would he or she say? But always remember: Everything that is said should move the story toward the ultimate end.

DIALECT

Frequently writers wish to use dialect to give the reader the flavor of the region or the character. *Use dialect sparingly.* If you have a character who drops *g*s let him drop a few, then use the dialogue for this character in the same way as any other, dropping an occasional *g* to remind the reader of this habit. Your reader will take care of the rest by dropping the *g* every time the character is in conversation. Dialect becomes tedious and tiresome. It tires your reader. And this frequent reader has been known to stop reading, or at the very least skim, painful stretches of dialect. Dialect can also force the reader to lose the continuity of the story and postpone finishing it.

THINKING AND SPEAKING

Many times a character is thinking rather than speaking a particular set of lines. Thinking should not be indicated by quotation marks. Quotes are reserved strictly for speaking and dialogue. Italics are frequently used to indicate thoughts in books. Many authors feel it is useful and (since the advent of the modern computer) necessary to indicate the thoughts with italics. Some editors still do not wish to see italics in manuscripts, but most are now computer savvy enough to accept italics.

"SAID"

Authors occasionally feel that "said" becomes tedious in a long string of dialogue. This problem is solved in several ways. First, it is not always necessary to identify the speaker after the initial pieces of conversation. For example, if there are only two characters involved in the conversation:

> "That's not true," Joe said.
> "You know it is," Allison shouted.
> "_____" (This will be Joe speaking.)
> "_____" (This will be Allison's dialogue.)

Alternating paragraphs will belong to each of the speakers and need not be indicated by "said Joe" and so on. This format shouldn't be continued longer than two-thirds of a page, lest the reader forget who is speaking and resort to counting lines. Remember: Whenever speakers change, a new paragraph should begin. Occasionally, new writers will want to pile several lines of dialogue into one paragraph. Remember your high school English teacher? New thought, *new paragraph*.

A second way of eliminating the dread of *said* is by adding taglines:

> Flipping her hair over her shoulder, she added, "You've always been so hateful."
> "And you are a liar," he snarled.

The flipping of the hair is a tagline used to give the reader a feeling for the action in the story. It also gives the reader an indication of the speaker without adding Allison's name to the dialogue. Taglines can be as boring as *said* if carried to extremes. When used sparingly they add action and emphasis to what might otherwise be a dull conversation. They are also a great tool to reveal a character's quirks or habits.

Dialogue is an excellent avenue for relating an important piece of information that occurs "offstage" or in the past but is necessary for the understanding of the story. For example, "I think Jim's been afraid of the water ever since he fell out of the boat that summer at Lake Dillon." Such a piece of information could be important later in the story when Jim fails to dive into the river to save a drowning child.

THINGS TO REMEMBER

- Dialogue should move the story forward.
- Dialogue reads quicker than narrative and therefore speeds up the pace of the writing.
- To test dialogue, read it out loud; or better yet, get someone else to read it to you.
- When faced with using narrative versus dialogue, *always* choose dialogue.

☞ EXERCISE

Use dialogue in your story to show more of your character and move the story along.

SELECTED READING

For dialogue that moves the story well and gives the reader insight into the characters, I recommend the following:

- Manuel Ramos's *The Ballad of Rocky Ruiz* (Evanston, IL: Northwestern University Press, 2003) for excellent use of dialect without interrupting the story
- John Steinbeck's *The Grapes of Wrath* (New York: Penguin Books, 2006)

SUMMARY

Dialogue can be duplicated by listening to people. Dialogue should help the storyline advance to the ultimate conclusion of the story. Dialect should be used sparingly. Thinking should be italicized, not put in quotation marks. *Said* can be alternated with taglines for a better story. New speakers require new paragraphs.

⑨

NARRATIVE

We have discussed dialogue and characterization, as well as some of the other necessities of a good story. I have purposely avoided discussing narrative until this point because most beginners use *too much* narrative and tend to lose readers in the very beginning due to this tendency.

Oh, how we struggle with narrative. Not only do beginners labor with the problem, but someone (who should be tarred and feathered) led writers to believe that it's okay to write in the omniscient viewpoint when writing narrative. What ensued was a giant leap backward for the writing profession and writers everywhere. The following are some thoughts and explanations on narrative.

1. Good narrative is an important part of any story. Stories composed only of dialogue tend to be tedious and difficult to read.
2. Narrative needs to move the story along and give depth to the story by adding description, setting, and action.
3. *Show the story—never tell it*. This is the cardinal rule of writing and it ultimately breaks many beginners. The big-screen-TV explanation is the best way of understanding the difference. Think of your story on the big screen—see the action, the characters, and the story on the screen.

Let the characters show the story with emotion and the five senses: hearing, seeing, smelling, tasting, and feeling. The reader should always have the sense that they are there with the character (ideally inside his or her head) experiencing the action with him or her.

Right:

> She glanced around the large room, scanning the loaded bookshelves that touched the ceiling on three sides, as the butler led her into the writer's study. She positioned herself on the edge of the brocade loveseat and checked her lipstick in the reflection from the well-polished coffee table in front of her. [Now you are inside of the character and experiencing the room from her viewpoint.]

Wrong:

> She was led into a library. Tall bookshelves stood on three sides of the room. In the center, a green brocade loveseat stood next to a well-polished coffee table. She sat down. [Now you are telling the story. Your character has become a plastic doll being pushed through your special playhouse by an omniscient voice.]

The difference is subtle but important. Read the examples again if necessary.

WRITING "SHOWING" NARRATIVE

Writing narrative is a matter of viewpoint. Here are the necessary aspects of narrative viewpoint writing:

1. Decide who your main viewpoint character is. Who owns the story's problem? This is the viewpoint character who will carry the majority of the story and your narrative.
2. Let your reader experience the story through the main character; this experience is the focal point of your narrative. If you want to describe the country setting, do it from your character's viewpoint. If something smells like home-baked cookies, have the character smell the odor. These experiences give the reader the feeling of being involved in the story.

Beginning writers have a tendency to interject their own opinions and philosophy into their works of fiction. Some advice: Don't! If you feel strongly about a subject and it fits within the context of your story, have it become the idea/philosophy of your character. Whatever you do, *stay out of your story*. Let your main character voice the opinions, thoughts, and philosophies. Remember it's all about *viewpoint*.

3. Some clever writer thought that seeing the story from varied viewpoints in separate paragraphs was brilliant. It is not! Once you've pulled your reader into the story with a viewpoint, stay with that viewpoint. If you find it necessary to add another point of view, start another chapter or at the very least center ### or ••• below the paragraph and insert an extra line space. This will give the reader at least some warning that things are changing.

SOME THOUGHTS

"Telling not showing" stands as the major difficulty uncovered in manuscripts submitted to the National Writers Association. Of the hundreds of book and short story manuscripts we see monthly and yearly, "telling" stands as the most common and the most deadly blunder. Telling will kill a manuscript with an editor in seconds. Every writer not only needs to be aware of this problem but must constantly be alert to recognize and to kill it before it's even born. It is an easy mode to slip into. Occasionally I find slips in my own work. It is a death knell for work seeking a publisher.

One easy way to avoid the "telling" pitfall is to make sure your work uses the five senses to the fullest extent. Make the character feel, see, hear, smell, and taste the world around him or her. The second way is to make anger, happiness, sorrow, despair, and every other emotion become a part of the story. Good writing has the ability to allow the reader to experience the story and figuratively become the main character without really noticing that's what's happening.

Stay in an active voice (tense, or whatever you wish to call it). From time to time, I have been caught calling this the present tense, but this is not necessarily accurate. Westerns and historical sagas are told in an

---

☞ **EXERCISE**

Write a paragraph or two in your story that has narrative (seen through the eyes of the character) and elaborates on the setting of the story.

---

active but past tense. Just don't fall into the pit of writing the story in the past tense because it is set in the past. Your reader needs to feel as a part of the story, and if you use past tense to write the story, the reader feels no impetus to become involved in what is going on and therefore to even finish the book.

SELECTED READINGS

Narrative has the unfortunate habit of making or breaking a story. For good narrative, I recommend the following:

- Gary Paulsen's *Hatchet* (New York: Puffin Books, 1987)
- Any Ann Rule book for outstanding nonfiction narrative

SUMMARY

Perfect the showing versus telling aspects of your writing by making sure you are in the main character's head and seeing the world through your character's eyes. Use the five senses and the gamut of human emotions to keep showing the story. Your reader wants and needs to become involved in the story. Stay in the active voice.

10

GLITCHES

This chapter might well be called "Catchall" or "Writing's Little Problems." It contains some of the most important information for a writer and yet is probably one of the easiest to forget or ignore. Entire books have been devoted to some of these principles, but beginning writers neglect them, and advanced writers forget they're even doing them.

If memory joggers, or mnemonic devices, are the way you remember, then think of SF TAPES. SF TAPES stands for "Setting, Flashbacks, Transitions, Action, Point of View, Emotion, and Style." These small glitches distinguish between the professionals and the beginners—the sold and the great masses of unsold writers.

SETTING

In the past, setting was an important part of any story. Today, it still comprises an important part of the story but is not as important as in previous eras. Where your story takes place is a key to the flavor of the story. Why is a story set in Chicago or Los Angeles or New York?

Recently, I was given the opportunity to be the final judge in a contest of already published works. Two of the books were outstanding, the third was passable, and the fourth was a poorly written novel that shouldn't have made it past the first judging except that the setting was a fascinating part of the story, and for some of the initial judges, I suspect the setting fooled them into thinking the novel was outstanding. The passable novel could have been set anywhere. This sad fact detracted from the writing and made the book only passable in the opinion of the other judges and me.

Setting is used for flavor in much the same way fresh cilantro makes outstanding salsa. This does not mean the author is supposed to lull the reader to sleep by long, meaningless descriptions. When a character enters a room, a complete description of every piece of furniture, drapery, rugs, and architecture is not necessary. However, if the blue velvet loveseat reminds him of his aunt Effie's Victorian parlor, then put it in. San Diego smells and sounds different from Denver, New York, or Chicago. Let your reader experience the setting, but don't describe every building, smell, or sound. Do give the reader a feel for the place and time. Setting adds flavor, believability, and reality to your story.

FLASHBACKS

The major reason for a flashback is to give the reader information he or she needs to understand the motivations of the characters. If your main character witnesses a child falling into the river and hesitates to rescue the child, a flashback to a time when he or she nearly drowned learning to swim gives the reader the information necessary to understand why the character doesn't dive right in.

Flashbacks can be several sentences long or a quick glimpse midsentence, such as the previous reference to Aunt Effie's loveseat. It should always be used to give the reader information necessary to the story or to add a unique flavor to the story. Setting off a long flashback with an extra line space gives the reader a warning that something is changing in the story and keeps him or her "with you" in the change. It is also acceptable to use three asterisks (°°°) or three pound signs (###) centered and set apart by extra line spaces.

Most flashbacks are written in the past perfect tense, which gives the reader a feeling for the action happening in the past. Flashbacks can also be written as a stream of consciousness. Never make a flashback longer than it needs to be. Getting off on a "tangent" by telling the reader every movement of the character's life since birth is not necessary. This holds the story in limbo for too long and bores the reader. Flashbacks are like the music played over the phone when you're on hold—fine for a while but eventually irritating.

Flashbacks should *never* be used to tell an entire story or a novel. If the novel or story needs to be told in the past, then set it in the past and go on with the story.

TRANSITIONS

Transitions are necessary when the scene, setting, action, point of view, or characters change. When possible, transitions should take place between chapters. This is especially true when changing the viewpoint character. Sudden shifts in viewpoint are very disconcerting and leave the reader confused and disoriented unless the writer gives a bit of warning. Viewpoint shifts, because they are momentous in nature, should always be reserved for a new chapter. This transition is accepted readily by the reader, where changing viewpoint within the chapter is difficult to follow.

A word of caution here. Some writers feel they can change viewpoint within a paragraph. Unless you've figured out a way to squeeze two brains into that one little skull, *don't do it.* This is basic high school English class here; when the speaker or thinker changes, you need a new paragraph and probably a new chapter. Scene, action, or setting changes can be made "reader friendly" by signaling them with an extra line space, thereby giving the reader a warning that something new is about to take place. Rough transitions make for difficult reading, and, therefore you may lose your reader. Avoid using one speaker in dialogue and another person thinking within the same paragraph. At least a paragraph transition is necessary.

ACTION

Action moves the story forward. For the beginning writer, we are not discussing a shooting or a fistfight or even a wild chase scene on every page. Any character movement is considered action. It can be something as simple as a nervous shift in a chair to the runaway locomotive charging down a steep incline. Action is necessary. Think about a single character lying on a field of daisies, musing about the philosophical state of the world. Are you going to read 200 pages of this? You may read some out of curiosity, but finishing 200 pages becomes a Herculean task. *Action* is necessary.

POINT OF VIEW

Again, let me stress the importance of viewpoint. Whose story is it? The story needs to belong to someone. Someone needs to *own* the problem. And that someone needs to solve the problem at the end. "Well," retorts the novice. "I am writing this from the omnipotent point of view." Fine. Is it everybody's story? Does everyone own the problem? Is everyone going to solve the problem? *Whose story is it?*

In most published novels or short stories, one character carries the story. Several characters may have a hand in the action or at times give their view of what is happening, but still one of the characters always remains as the major leader of the action and dialogue. This character is the main character, or the viewpoint character. Shifts away from this character should be handled carefully and with a distinct shift well delineated to the reader. Many novels and short stories I have read for different contests have the most problem when it comes to viewpoint and viewpoint characters.

Some Things to Remember About Viewpoint

1. Short stories are not long enough for multiple viewpoints. Decide who the story "belongs to" and stick with him or her for the viewpoint character.
2. Possible viewpoints include
   - First person, "I" viewpoint: This is an excellent mode if you do not want your reader to know what others in the story are thinking. Until recently, novels rarely used the "I" viewpoint, but it is

becoming more popular and has some valid usage in certain situations. The "I" technique is an excellent one to use when writing a mystery because the killer never needs to enter into the viewpoint character's thoughts.

- Second person, "you" viewpoint: A strange creature, indeed, but the best-selling prizewinning novel *Bright Lights, Big City* by Jay McInereny was written in the "you" viewpoint.
- Third person, "he, she, or it" viewpoint: Third person viewpoint is the best choice for writing. Research has shown that the reader takes on the persona of the main character if the author uses *he* or *she* as much as possible in the story. Third person takes on three features:

  a. Objective, where the writer reports what he or she senses about the characters and action
  b. Subjective, where the writer goes in and out of the minds and emotions of the characters
  c. Personal, where the writer enters the persona of one of the characters and tells the whole story from that person's viewpoint.

Number three is my personal favorite because it gives the story focus. It is also the most valid viewpoint for a short story.

Most writers should avoid turning the third person into an omniscient viewpoint. The omniscient viewpoint is extremely difficult to write well. Generally, what occurs is that the writer lapses into telling rather than showing the story. Remember: The old spy camera in the corner doesn't work well in fiction.

Some Thoughts

Even in novels switches in viewpoint should be placed in different chapters or, at the very least, should be clearly delineated with an extra line space to prepare the reader for a new scene and a new view of the action. If not handled well, switches in viewpoint can be very disturbing to the reader. Numerous or poorly defined viewpoint switches lose the reader, and this means the reader may put the material down, never to return. *Never lose your reader.*

> ☞ **EXERCISE**
>
> Use what you have learned about flashbacks, transitions, and other elements to incorporate a flashback into your story. Remember that the flashback should have a smooth transition in and out of your story and should give information about the character without slowing down the story's pace.

EMOTION

How do you manage to get your reader involved in the story? Once you have your hook and the reader is anxious to get on with the story, how do you keep him or her reading? The answer is *emotion*. We all laugh, cry, love, hate, get angry, and have moments of happiness unless we have been dehumanized to the level of robots. Emotion is the universal tie between all humans—and the writer's greatest friend. Allowing the reader to become involved in the story through the commonality of emotion is a key to keeping that reader interested. Reach readers through their eyes and feelings. *The reader's heart is the writer's open door.*

STYLE

Just because style has been saved for last doesn't in any way indicate its lack of importance. My words on style are few: Use your own! Style brings clarity, coherence, and unity to your work. Don't copy someone else's style because it has brought them success. One of the saddest conversations I remember having involved a young writer who called me and said, "I've read everything that John Irving has ever written and now I am going to write like John Irving." My advice was, the world already has John Irving and we enjoy him, but we don't need another one. Write like *you*.

SELECTED READINGS

For setting, I recommend

- Maggie Osborne's *Emerald Rain* (New York: St. Martin's Press, 1991)
- John Stith's *Redshift Rendezvous* (Rockville, MD: Wildside Press, 2001)
- Stephen White's *Private Practices* (New York: Viking, 1993)

For flashbacks, I recommend

- Joanne Greenberg's *I Never Promised You a Rose Garden* (New York: New American Library, 2004)
- Lee Karr's *The Housesitter* (New York: Avon Books, 1980)

For transitions, I recommend

- Diane Mott Davidson's *Dying for Chocolate* (New York: Bantam Books, 1992)
- Connie Willis's *Lincoln's Dreams* (New York: Bantam Books, 1987)

For action, I recommend

- Any Mary Higgins Clark book
- Stephen Coonts's *Flight of the Intruder* (Annapolis, MD: Naval Institute Press, 2006)
- Any book by Clive Cussler
- Joseph Wambaugh's *The Blue Knight* (Boston: Little, Brown, 1972)

Viewpoint is a difficult call; any good author must be highly cognizant of viewpoint if they intend to stay in the business. I recommend reading several books with more than one viewpoint in order to get a "feel" for the technique.

For emotion, I recommend

- Doris Betts's *Souls Raised From the Dead* (New York: Knopf, 1994)
- John Irving's *A Prayer for Owen Meany* (New York: Modern Library, 2002)
- Any Ann Rule book
- Nicholas Sparks's *The Rescue* (New York: Warner Books, 2000)

SUMMARY

Setting gives your writing flavor and interest, but use it sparingly. References to setting should move the story along and add reality to the story. Flashbacks give the reader important information. A whole novel or short story should not be told as a flashback. Transitions in a novel should be well defined and, if they are significant, should be placed in new chapters. Action moves the story forward and is necessary to every piece. Action propels the reader through the pages. The person who "owns the problem" is your point-of-view character. Short stories can only have one viewpoint. Generally, shifts in viewpoint in the same paragraph (sometimes in the same sentence) are the mark of an amateur and will tag your work as such in the eyes of editors. Romance writing is the exception to the rule regarding viewpoint shifts. Romance writers frequently shift viewpoints in the same paragraph, and this is accepted by both readers and publishers. It is suggested that beginning writers use caution when falling into this habit. Emotion is the universal thread that ties the reader to the writer. Emotion gets and keeps the reader involved in the story. Style brings clarity, coherence, and unity to your work—use your own style.

NONFICTION

Ask any professional writer, and most of them will tell you that they enjoy writing fiction but make more money writing nonfiction. At one point the two areas were mutually exclusive; now, however, nonfiction writers are allowed to cross the golden barriers and write fiction. In recent years several of the highly touted fiction books were written by authors who already had published nonfiction books. So if you want to write fiction but begin in the dungeon of nonfiction, it does not necessarily mean you will be forever condemned there.

One of the questions that constantly surfaces when discussing nonfiction is "How much research do I need to do?" The answer to that is "As much as you feel is necessary." Do you have a command of the subject? Are you comfortable interviewing experts on the subject? Do you recognize most of the terms and expressions common to the subject? Could you carry on an easy conversation with a knowledgeable person in the field? If the answers to these questions are *yes*, then your research is complete and you are ready to write.

TYPES OF NONFICTION ARTICLES

Because there are thousands of nonfiction publications, there are thousands of markets for articles. These range from information on cooking a dinner for two to highly technical articles on global information systems. Most articles fall into one of the following categories:

1. How-to: This can be anything from crocheting an afghan to building a nuclear missile. Anyone reading this book has expertise in areas that others may not have. Why not share that knowledge with a how-to?
2. Jump essay: These fall into the catchall of fillers, humor, and from seeing and remembering to the sharing of thoughts on a particular subject. Most op-ed (opinion-editorial) pieces are jump essays.
3. Journal: Most journaling is for personal use, but occasionally the journal technique can be used for "a day in the life of" or for chronicles of the famous or terminally ill.
4. Incident with a purpose: Used for emotional response. Whether it is the "Can This Marriage Be Saved?" or "Young Mother's Story," the incident with a purpose is widely read and popular. The writing of the incident takes on this format:
   - Recall the incident.
   - Why is it worth remembering?
   - Discover the point.
   - Write as rapidly as possible.
   - Examine the story and then set it aside.
   - After a short period pull out and revise.
5. Nostalgic essay: Currently are enjoying a resurgence. This is a typical "I remember when" essay.
6. Here and now experience: A significant event that occurred in your life or someone else's life. The famous *Reader's Digest's* "Drama in Real Life" section is typical of these types of stories.
7. Interview: Local celebrities and the rich, famous, or infamous are likely candidates for interviews. Many small newspapers like interviews of new business owners or local civic leaders for their pages. Be sure to have your interview questions well thought out before going to the interview. The interview may take an interesting turn,

but don't count on this turn of events to make a lively story. Some writers prefer to record interviews. You should always be certain you have permission to record your interviewee. I advise getting this permission in writing. A boilerplate permission form can be found in Appendix J.

8. Profile: Can be written without a lengthy interview of the subject but usually has a focal point, such as those that appear on celebrity cooks or some other forum.

TECHNICAL AND BUSINESS WRITING

If you have skills in business or a technical expertise, the fields of business and technical writing are probably the most open for new freelancers. Anyone who has ever prayed for an interpreter for a computer manual wishes it was written by ordinary people instead of programmers. If you can write in a clear, concise, and sequential manner, the technical field needs you.

Many businesses wish to reach the public with press releases, media events, or just well-written letters or advertising copy. Freelance business writers are in demand, especially by small companies who cannot afford to hire a person to take care of this task or do not have the money to hire a public relations firm.

SUMMARY

Nonfiction is an excellent way to pay the bills. There are thousands of publications looking for nonfiction pieces. Most nonfiction falls into the categories of how-to, jump essay, journal, incident with a purpose,

---

☞ EXERCISE

Write a brief paragraph of nonfiction. If you are writing a short story, as your continuing exercise, develop a brief autobiographical paragraph.

nostalgic essay, here and now experience, interview, or profile. If you have business or technical expertise, there are writing jobs available in these areas, where other areas may be closed to new writers.

SELECTED READINGS

The following authors write some of the most readable nonfiction possible: Dee Brown, Harry MacLean, Ann Rule, and Thomas Thompson. Also for writers interested in articles, I suggest the following:

- Bonnie Hearn's *Focus Your Writing* (Redding, CA: CT Publishing, 1995)
- Eva Shaw's *The Successful Writer's Guide to Publishing Magazine Articles* (Loveland, CO: Rogers and Nelsen, 1998)

INTERNET PUBLISHING

Almost any author can obtain quick publication on the Internet. This may satisfy the writer's need for credits, but some cautionary advice should be heeded:

1. Although thousands of Internet magazines and book publishers are available on the World Wide Web, many do not pay.
2. Copyright encryption software is currently available but is not widely used by Internet publishers. This makes your Internet-published works vulnerable to piracy and plagiarism. A humor column from one of my friends, Bruce Cameron, has appeared in at least three forms on my e-mail from three different sources. Ultimately, it is still Bruce's column, although nowhere is it attributed to him.
3. Like the stigma of vanity and self-publishing in the past, many in the book publishing world see Internet publishing as purely an ego trip and not an authentic published work because many Internet publishers edit the material sparingly or do not edit it at all.

INTERNET BOOK SELF-PUBLISHING

Internet book self-publishing offers writers an inexpensive, easy, and quick way to become published. However, it is not without its pitfalls. One author I know placed his book with an Internet publisher five years ago. Because the only way a reviewer could obtain a copy was to pay for and download the book, it received no reviews despite hundreds of post-cards the author sent to book review editors. To date he has sold one book.

Recently a copy of a contract from an Internet publisher crossed my desk. The publisher was requiring "all rights throughout the universe, into perpetuity." There go your chances to publish on Mars or anywhere else on this planet for that matter. If your purpose in Internet self-publishing is to attract a "hardback or paperback" publisher, then don't sign away those rights. Be sure the contract you are signing is what you *really* want.

Some Internet publishers are now offering print-on-demand (POD) services in addition to e-publishing. This situation is closer to the ideal than anything previously available. The author should make sure he or she is able to receive at least 20 author copies of the book for personal use, as well as obtain the publisher's promise (in writing, in the contract) to send a number of copies (more than 100) for review.

Make sure that your Internet POD book has all the makings of a "real" book. These include ISBN, UPC number, LC (Library of Congress Cataloguing-in-Progress) number, and a copyright page with all pertinent information included. Authors choosing POD should also be aware that major bookstore chains, such as Barnes and Noble, will not ordinarily stock the books on their shelves because there is no provision for returning the books if they do not sell.

☞ **EXERCISE**

Search the Internet and find at least 10 Internet publishers (magazine or book) who accept and publish your type of material. Note if they are paying markets.

SUMMARY

Internet publishing for both short and book-length works is now available, but the author should be aware of pitfalls. Currently, much work on the Internet is vulnerable to plagiarism and piracy. If you decide to self-publish or do a POD Internet book, make certain the finished product looks like a regular book.

13

RIGHTS AND COPYRIGHT

Perhaps no other phase of the writing process is more misunderstood or misinterpreted than the areas of rights and copyright. What follows is not a total delineation of this area but should offer some basic guidelines for the writer when approaching this matter.

SHOULD I PUT THE COPYRIGHT SYMBOL IN THE UPPER RIGHT-HAND CORNER OF MY MANUSCRIPT?

Perhaps this question is best approached by discussing the reaction of editors to seeing the symbol on the manuscript. Most editors feel it is an affront to suggest that they may need to be reminded that your work is copyrighted. The suggestion that the author needs to remind the editor of copyright law also infers that the editor is going to steal the work or portions of it for his or her own uses—not a nice way to begin a relationship between strangers, especially one in which the author seeks to gain a long-term, mutually beneficial connection. Due to the volume of manuscripts received weekly by even the smallest publication, it is highly unlikely that an editor would "steal" your work.

ISN'T IT NECESSARY FOR THE EDITOR TO KNOW THE WORK IS COPYRIGHTED?

Most editors are exceedingly familiar with the current copyright laws. In October 1976, Public Law 94-553 was signed by President Ford. This law essentially states that statutory copyright protection extends for both published and unpublished works from the moment of their "creation." For the purposes of this law, *creation* is defined as "the moment the work is in a fixed, tangible or non-transitory form; in the case of unpublished or yet-to-be-published manuscripts, this would mean the final draft or final copy." This law reduces the significance of publication and grants protection for the work from the moment of the work's creation.

WHY FILE A COPYRIGHT FORM IF THE WORK IS PROTECTED ONCE IT IS CREATED?

Currently the law states that your work is protected; however, should an infringement occur and you decide to pursue litigation regarding the infringement, the work must be registered in order to satisfactorily proceed with court action.

IF I WANT TO LEGALLY COPYRIGHT MY WORK, WHAT DO I DO?

For written work an author must obtain a TX form from the Copyright Office, Library of Congress, Washington, DC 20559. The form can also be downloaded from the Library of Congress website. Compared to previous versions of this form, the current form is relatively easy to understand and fill out. For an unpublished manuscript, one complete copy of the work and a $45 fee should accompany the TX form. For published works, two copies of the completed book and $45 fee should accompany the form.

WHAT IF MY WORK IS NOT A MANUSCRIPT BUT A RECORDING OR VISUAL ART?

Forms are available for all types of work. You need only to request the proper form. The types and uses are as follows:

- *Form PA* is used for all published and unpublished works of performing arts, such as dramatic, musical, or audiovisual works.
- *Form VA* is used for copyrighting visual arts works, such as pictorial, graphic, or sculptural work.
- *Form SR* is necessary for sound recordings.
- *Form RE* is the form necessary for renewing previously copyrighted works already in their first term when the new law was enacted in 1976.
- *Form CA* is used as a clarification form to correct any errors on a previous registration.
- *Form GR/CP* is for a group registration for contributions to periodicals. This form should be used in conjunction with one of the other basic forms when several pieces have been used within a twelve-month period.
- *Form SE* is used for serial publications, such as magazines or newspapers.

WHAT DOES COPYRIGHT PROTECTION MEAN TO ME?

Under the present law, all materials registered by copyright are protected for the life of the author plus 70 years. As the owner of the copyright, you have certain protection and rights not granted to any other user of the work. The protection guards against the infringement or piracy of your work. You are also granted certain rights, which include the right to produce copies of the work; the right to prepare derivative works; the right to distribute copies of the work by sale, transfer of ownership, rental, lease, or lending; the right to publicly perform the work; and the right to publicly display the work.

WHAT IS "FAIR USE" AND HOW DOES IT AFFECT ME AS A WRITER?

Perhaps one of the most nebulous laws regarding copyright centers around the subject of "fair use." According to the fair-use doctrine, portions of another author's work can be used in your work if it does not constitute a significant amount of the work. If the work is one paragraph— one sentence could constitute a significant amount. If the work is book length, one page may not form a significant amount. National Writers Association suggests that authors should limit use of others' works to less than one page if the work is book length, but all numbers are arbitrary. The following guidelines may assist the confused writer regarding fair use:

1. Whether the purpose and character of the use is commercial or nonprofit and educational
2. The nature of the copyrighted work, whether it is a manuscript or a play and so forth
3. The effect of the use on the potential market
4. The amount of the work used in comparison to the work as a whole

If you are concerned about the amount of another work you are quoting, it is always advisable to contact the publisher and the author of the work you are quoting.

MY PUBLISHER WANTS TO COPYRIGHT MY WORK IN HIS NAME. WHAT'S WRONG WITH THAT?

For your particular purposes, maybe nothing. You will, in the case of a book, continue to collect royalties for your lifetime. However, upon your death, a publisher can continue to publish your work, and your heirs or your estate may receive nothing from the publication.

I'VE HEARD THERE ARE THINGS YOU CAN'T COPYRIGHT. WHAT ARE THEY?

Some authors are shocked to find there are things you cannot copyright. Here are a few:

1. Ideas: You may have the best idea in the world, but you cannot copyright an idea.
2. Titles: Yes, it is possible to write another *Gone With the Wind*. Titles do not fall under copyright protection.
3. Work-made-for-hire: Any work created while under the employment of another is considered work-for-hire and cannot be copyrighted by the creator unless specific provisions were made prior to the creation to allow for this.
4. Procedures, processes, systems, methods of operation, concepts, principles, or discoveries, regardless of the form in which they are described, explained, illustrated, or embodied: This is not a definitive work and is not copyrightable.

WHAT ARE THE LAWS REGARDING MY WORK ON THE INTERNET?

As stated in the Internet chapter, encryption software is currently available. However, most Internet publishers do not use it, and this makes your work vulnerable to piracy and plagiarism. (Note explanation of copyright law. For specific questions of doubt, contact National Writers Association at (303) 841-0246 for further explanation or referral to a copyright attorney.)

LITERARY RIGHTS

Once you have created a work, you have the option and right to sell that work. Unlike copyright, which is rather straightforward at this point, which rights to sell can be confusing and unclear. The simplest way to determine which rights should be sold is to ask yourself why and for whom the work was created.

Is the work a one-time shot for a specific market? Is it possible that you will not want to spin off other works from the research you have used for this piece? If the work is for a specific market and can't be spun off or reused, then you may want to sell *all rights*. Remember: In doing this you will no longer own the piece and have no right to use any of the material after the specific market has used the piece. Generally it is not recommended that you sell all rights. If you do determine that you are willing to sell all rights, be sure that the payment you receive is fair compensation for the amount of work necessary to produce the piece. As a general rule, publications purchasing all rights tend to be some of the lowest paying in the market.

One-time rights mean the purchaser is paying you to use the piece one time, after which all rights to the piece revert back to you. This means no other stipulations or restrictions are placed on the work.

First serial rights mean the periodical is purchasing the piece to use *first* in its publication. No other publication may print the piece until the purchasing periodical has used it. The term *serial* is a reference to a serial publication, such as a magazine or newspaper, not that they are serializing the piece.

First North American serial rights are the most ideal rights to sell because this means the publisher can only use the piece in periodicals published in North America. If the periodical has a Latin American issue or a European issue, then he or she must pay additionally to purchase these rights. Some magazines prefer to purchase *first world rights*. This cuts out your ability to sell the piece to the same magazine for their other language editions.

First rights are a variation of the previously mentioned rights but generally give the publisher the right to print the piece in whatever medium he or she wishes and in other versions (Spanish, Australian) of the work.

Simultaneous rights mean the work may be printed at the same time other publications print it. These are sold with religious publications or in a newspaper's Sunday magazine where the circulation does not overlap. This term is sometimes used instead of one-time rights.

Syndication rights are sold when a piece will be sold to newspaper syndicates. This means the piece will most probably appear in several newspapers at the same time. Book publishers will purchase syndication rights if they are serializing a book in a magazine or newspaper.

Reprint rights indicate the piece has been sold once and is being offered to a different market for publication. Many authors, using reprint rights, recycle their short stories and articles to a variety of publications.

BOOK RIGHTS

Each book contract is different but can contain sections referring to a variety of rights. Rights most commonly negotiated by publishers include hardcover, mass market paperback, trade paperback, book club, sequel, audio, anthology, condensation, revised edition, and limited edition. Rights usually handled by agents include dramatic rights, foreign rights, translation rights, and some merchandising and character rights. A word of caution: Book contracts can and may carry some nonauthor-slanted language on the rights issues or other important points. It is strongly suggested you contact a literary agent, a copyright attorney, or National Writers Association before signing a book contract.

At this writing, the issue of electronic rights for all works—long and short—are of concern. Because the copyright law does not address this issue adequately, many authors may find their works jeopardized by placing the works or portions of them on online bulletin board services. Authors should approach these venues with extreme caution.

SUMMARY

Copyright is a complex area. Beginning writers need to know that their work is copyrighted from the moment of "creation," but litigation on infringement cannot take place unless the copyright is registered on a TX form with the Copyright Office. Editors, for the most part, don't have the time or the inclination to plagiarize work. Copyright is in effect for the life of the author, plus 70 years. Fair use addresses the purpose and character of the usage, plus the nature of the work, effect on the market, and amount of the work used.

When selling your work, it is recommended that you sell one-time or first North American serial rights. Book rights involve hardcover, mass market, trade, book club, serial or sequel, audio, anthology, condensation, and revised and limited editions. Book contract rights should always be carefully and knowledgeably negotiated.

⑭

QUERIES, SYNOPSES, COVER LETTERS, PROPOSALS, AND OUTLINES

When you have your research done or have several chapters of a book written, you need to begin considering which markets are most likely to be interested in your work. At this point you will want to construct a query letter to possible markets and perhaps a chapter-by-chapter outline if you are writing a nonfiction book. Marketing is covered in the next chapter, but at this point a discussion of queries, synopses, cover letters, proposals, and outlines is in order.

QUERIES

Keep in mind that queries are necessary only for books and articles. Short stories do not need a query but can be sent in their entirety to the chosen market. Most beginning writers are unsure of what to include in a query letter and just how to go about writing one. Your query letter is a selling tool. I hear the protests now: "I don't want to be a salesperson. I want to write!" Whether you want to be a salesperson or not, if you intend to sell your work, you will need to become a salesperson. Who better to sell your work than you? You know your work better than anyone.

It is your brainchild. You know its weaknesses and strengths. *No one* can sell your work better than you can. So let's get to it!

The standard query letter should not take up more than one page single spaced. A neat, professional stationery sheet is an added plus, but if you do not have your own stationery yet, use standard 8½"-by-11" typing paper in white or beige. When you are ready for professional stationery, most professional writers caution against using the words *freelance writer* in the header. This may turn off the editor rather than having the desired effect. No fancy colors or insignias are necessary.

The body of the query should consist of the first paragraph as a hook. If you have a good hook on your article, use it in the letter. The editor reading your query needs some reason to read on, just as he or she will need a reason to read your entire article. See Appendix D for a sample query letter.

The second paragraph tells the editor exactly why you think this piece is right for this publication. The paragraph may also contain exactly what you are prepared to offer the magazine—one article of _____ words; several black and white photographs or color slides; a sidebar if it is appropriate; and graphs, charts, or other illustrations that will assist the reader in understanding the content of your article. Giving the editor the option of photos, graphs, illustrations, and the probable word count tells that editor that you are thinking of his or her needs that are visually oriented, in addition to the printed word.

Paragraph three should give any special qualifications you have for writing this article in addition to research you may have done in order to write the piece. A concluding short paragraph thanking the editor for the time necessary to consider your proposal is always good etiquette. Be sure to include a self-addressed stamped envelope for the editor's reply.

If you have many writing credits you may want to include a vita sheet of your accomplishments with the query letter. Some publications will request "tearsheets." A tearsheet is a photocopy of an article written by the writer that may be similar to the ones the publication is known for publishing. If you don't have tearsheets, don't apologize or tell the editor you are just beginning; just make sure the article will stand on its own. If querying for a nonfiction book, you may be asked to include a chapter-by-chapter outline with your query.

OUTLINES

The length of a chapter outline will depend on the number of chapters in the book and the length of the book. Most outlines can cover approximately four chapters on each page of the outline. Using this book as an example, the following is the format that you should use.

Chapter 1: Getting Started

This chapter covers the necessity of having a certain place to write, what tools are necessary to begin writing, and the necessity of a daily routine.

Chapter 2: Ideas, Ideas, Ideas

Getting and keeping ideas is the subject of Chapter 2. Suggestions are given as to where writers can find ideas for their idea file and methods of storing ideas.

The chapter outline can be single spaced in each section, but extra line spaces should be used between chapter sections. See Appendix E for a sample chapter-by-chapter outline.

SYNOPSIS

Several calls per month to the National Writers Association deal with the subject of a synopsis. It is interesting that even the most professional writer has difficulty writing a synopsis. Points to consider when writing a synopsis are as follows:

1. The synopsis should not run more than four pages (single spaced) or 10 pages double spaced, unless otherwise required by the publisher or agent.
2. It can be single spaced.
3. It must tell the end of the story.
4. It should not be merely a cast of characters who are involved in the story.

The basic synopsis should tell your story. Tell the story to the editor in the same fashion you would tell a friend who asks you over a cup of coffee what your novel is about. Remember Chapter 9? This is the *only* place you can tell your story in narrative style. Appendix A contains a sample synopsis.

COVER LETTERS

It used to be unnecessary to write a cover letter for inclusion with a short story; however, the current trend in many magazines is to have the author write a letter to include with the submission of a short story. The letter should include a brief mention of the enclosed material and a one- to two-sentence bio about yourself that will be used at the end of the article. The cover letter should not run more than one-half to two-thirds of a page.

PROPOSALS

A book proposal, sometimes called a package, is used generally for non-fiction books. The proposal contains the query letter, an outline of the book in chapter-by-chapter format, the writer's vita or summary of other published work (not to exceed one page), a competitive analysis of other books available on the market, and a sample chapter or several chapters, depending on the desire of the editor or agent. The competitive analysis, sometimes called a market study, is an excellent idea with most non-fiction books because it shows that you are aware of the publishing company's challenge of determining whether the market will sustain another book on a given subject. It will also give them an idea of "who will buy this book," which is very important in the current publishing market.

☞ **EXERCISE**

Write a cover letter or query regarding the current short story, novel, or article you are producing.

Never send more chapters than the agent or editor requests. Always send successive chapters, preferably Chapters 1 and 2. The editor or agent wants to decide whether the author sustains a consistent theme and good writing.

SUGGESTED READING

- Michael Larsen's *How to Write a Book Proposal* (Cincinnati, OH: Writer's Digest Books, 2003)

SUMMARY

Queries are a selling tool used for nonfiction books and articles. They should "sell" the editor on your idea. *Outlines* are used to give the editor an idea about the contents of each chapter. A *synopsis* is a telling of a novel from beginning to end. *Cover letters* are used to introduce the editor to your short story. *Proposals* or *packages* include a query letter, chapter-by-chapter outline, writer's vita, competitive or market analysis, and as many sample chapters as are preferred by the editor.

⓯

THE WRITER AS AN EDITOR

You've crafted a story using every bit of knowledge you could glean from the material included in this book, critique groups, other books, and, for the brave, perhaps family members. You think you are ready to start sending your work to publishers. You take a breath, edge your toes closer to the rim of the pool, hold your nose—but *hold it*. You aren't quite as ready as you think you are. So take a couple of relieved steps back from the deep end and consider this: Even the most outstanding writers out there need to edit *one more time*.

Usually it is recommended that you put your manuscript away for at least a week, a month if possible, before you do a final edit. "Editing," you say smugly, "is what publishers pay their in-house editors for."

"*Wrong*, wrong, wrong," I tell you. "Maybe they did once upon a time, but no more." The days of publishing editors like Maxwell Perkins are gone. If you expect to make it *big* in this very competitive, very difficult field, you must put your best effort and presentation forward. For all his brilliance as a writer, Ernest Hemingway would have a difficult time making it in the current publishing world. (It's rumored his spelling was atrocious.) And the dragging pace of F. Scott Fitzgerald would never see print in today's market, either. Dickens would never make it to an editorial board, and Hawthorne would be the butt of assistant editors' lunch jokes. With the advent of big conglomerates ingesting larger publishers, a new kind of publishing house and editor is now on the scene. Publishing houses are now run by CEOs and business MBAs who are not devoted editors or, in some cases, not even editors who believe in good writing. Their bottom line is the financial one, and what they want are *commercial properties*. If a manuscript needs a deep edit, even if it is a highly marketable story, the likelihood that a large publishing house will buy it is somewhere around zero.

Armed with this information, you must be aware that your manuscript must be the very best manuscript submitted. Everyone has his or her own little quirks. Whether it is my downfall—I can't tell you how many editors have had to catch my spelling of *environment*—or the fact that you think the word *manila* not only rhymes with *vanilla* but is spelled the same way, it's a fact that editors have their pet peeves. A good computer spell-checker and, ultimately, an even better human spell-checker are necessary for a polished final draft.

What follows are the three rating sheets used by National Writers Association judges when rating entries in novel, short story, article and essay, and poetry contests. Each is self-explanatory in regard to content. What I am urging is that you consider that everything on these sheets goes into making your work a salable, finished product. Remember: You are the kindest, most understanding reader your work will have from now until publication, so be a little tough on yourself before a perfect stranger is.

FICTION CRITIQUE

100 possible points:

1. Overall appearance: proper manuscript format, type of paper, font and type readability, neatness and margins, grammar, syntax, spelling, punctuation (5 points)
2. Basic theme/idea: thematic statement, focus, consistency (2 points)
3. Plot/storyline: structure—dilemma/conflict/crises/climax/conclusion, effectiveness of the ending, originality or freshness of plot (12 points)

4. Characterization: quirks/traits, motivation, dimensions, background (12 points)
5. Description: detail, reaching reader through senses and sensations, use of images, symbols, freshness/originality (8 points)
6. Narration: showing versus telling, pace, transitions, fluidity, cliches, tone and mood. (15 points)
7. Dialogue: convincing/lifelike, use to reveal characters, handling of dialect (10 points)
8. Point of view: focus and control, told from best viewpoint, consistency (10 points)
9. Plausibility: well researched, believability of situation or characters, convincing, effectiveness of suspending reader's disbelief (3 points)
10. Reader interest: effectiveness of opening/hook, reader interest sustained (10 points)
11. Marketability: within the confines of the current market, is the manuscript marketable? (13 points)

Be honest with yourself here. If your score is below a 90, you need a major rewrite because your book or short story won't have a chance in the competitive market.

NONFICTION RATING CRITIQUE

100 possible points

1. Manuscript format (5 points)
2. Overall appearance (5 points)

   a) Quality of paper
   b) Quality of print
   c) Neatness, margins, etc.
   d) Grammar
   e) Spelling
   f) Punctuation

3. Title (3 points)
4. Is the work interesting? (2 points)

5. Is the idea fresh, original, or with a different slant? (5 points)
6. How do you rate the beginning/lead? (5 points)
7. Is the material or idea significant? (5 points)
8. Quality of the research? (10 points)
9. Does the author get the most out of the subject? (5 points)
10. Is there emotional appeal? (1 point)
11. Does the work teach, entertain, or have other redeeming features? (10 points)
12. Viewpoint: consistent, focused, told from the best viewpoint (10 points)
13. Style of writing (1 point)
14. Characterization (1 point)
15. Descriptions (2 points)
16. Narrative (5 points)
17. Transition and organization: Does it flow smoothly? (10 points)
18. Is the work too technical, too scholarly? (2 points)
19. How do you rate the graphics (if any)? (3 points)
20. On a scale of 1 (least possible) to 10, how do you rate its salability? (10 points)

Once again, 90 points is the magic number. If your piece won't rate at least a 90 out of 100, then you need to rewrite the piece or at least work on it a bit more.

POETRY CRITIQUE FORM

100 possible points

1. Format: grammar, spelling, punctuation, format on the page (includes neatness, light type, etc.) (10 points)
2. Clarity: Does the piece convey its message effectively? (15 points)
3. Flow: Do the words move the reader? (15 points)
4. Content (15 points)
5. Style: Is the poetic style consistent? (15 points)
6. Marketability (15 points)
7. Reader interest (15 points)

☞ **EXERCISE**

Use one of the three sheets to critique a piece of your own work. Try to think of the piece as belonging to someone else and rate the work. Locate your trouble spots and fix them.

SUMMARY

In order to provide a salable piece, the writer should be his or her own best editor. This includes more than just proofreading and should extend to all phases of the piece. The rating sheets will assist with developing and editing a more marketable work.

(16)

TO AGENT OR NOT TO AGENT

Let's concentrate on some of the pitfalls to avoid when taking your work into the marketplace, particularly regarding agents. If you are writing works of nonfiction or are selling to smaller publishers, you may not need an agent. If you wish to sell to larger publishers, you will absolutely need an agent, as most large publishers will not accept unagented submissions. In addition to this problem, large publishers have a legal department and contracts that require Perry Mason to read the fine print.

For a good indicator of whether a particular agent you are considering is a good choice, see if he or she is a member of the Association of Author's Representatives (AAR). Some outstanding agents are not members of the AAR, but many are. Many new agents have not sold enough work to be accepted into the AAR but may be accepted at a later date. AAR will not accept members who charge a reading fee. Some authors think nothing of using agents who charge reading fees, and many very legitimate agents are now asking for reading fees. However, consider these facts:

- Fact 1: Agents get literally hundreds of manuscripts weekly.
- Fact 2: If a fee-charging agent receives 20 manuscripts per week (a low estimate) and charges a $100 reading fee, that calculates to

$2,000 per week, $8,000 per month. That's $96,000 per year. Not a bad living when you consider he or she may not have sold even *one* manuscript.

- Fact 3: Agents are supposed to gain their income from *selling* your work, not reading it.

Check National Writers Association Research Report #51. Agents listed on this report have submitted questionnaires indicating a willingness to work with our members. We do not place agents on the list who charge more than minimal reading fees. Other places to look for agents include the Writer's Digest book *Guide to Literary Agents*, which is published yearly. You might also ask your writing friends who act as their agents. Some writers will tell you and others won't, but it never hurts to ask. If you attend conferences and seminars, ask the speakers who their agents are. Most conferences also invite agents to attend and meet with attendees. This is usually an excellent opportunity to find an agent.

DEALING WITH AGENTS

Here are a few things to keep in mind when dealing with agents. Agents are people. Occasionally, they have family problems, illnesses, and other things that slow down their progress. Treat them as fairly and respectfully as you want to be treated. Be patient and give them time to consider your work. Things to remember about the care and feeding of agents:

1. It is wise to query agents with a brief letter, a synopsis of your work, perhaps a chapter, and a #10 self-addressed, stamped envelope for their reply. Check the agent guidelines and find out what they want from you; then give them exactly what they want.

2. Do not send your manuscript and then call to find out if the agent has received it. If you want to know if the manuscript was received, enclose a postcard along with the manuscript for the agent to return to you when they receive the work.

3. Do not *call* agents. If they are busy negotiating a contract, your call could interrupt important discussions. Would you want some clod interrupting your agent, if he or she was on the telephone negotiating an important contract for *your* book? If you have an agent, I feel a brief bimonthly (that's every two months—not twice a month) call to inquire about status is not out of line. The buzz word here is *brief*, and it is wise to ascertain if the agent is amenable to this procedure.

4. When negotiating agent contracts, learn the parameters for your relationship. How often can you expect progress reports? Will you receive copies of the rejections from editors? (I recommend you request this. However, you should remember that agents are reluctant to do this when authors call the respective editors and *demand* to know why they didn't take the book.) You must assure the agent that you will be professional when dealing with these rejection letters and use them only for your own tracking purposes and for any constructive comments that might improve the material. If you are paying a portion of the expenses (I don't recommend over $200), when and how often will you receive reports on these expenditures? Request—no, insist—on a termination clause in your contract for the protection of both you and your agent. You need a way to end the relationship in a less than adversarial manner should it be necessary.

Finally, check with the National Writers Association office for advice or information about your prospective agent. Any agent who has warranted a number of member complaints should be approached with caution.

☞ **EXERCISE**

Go to the bookstore. Find books like yours, and check the acknowledgments page and a literary agents book to see if you can determine what agent represented the book. If the agent is interested in a certain kind of book, he or she may like yours. Write down these prospective agents' names, and see what you can learn about them besides their address.

SUMMARY

First, be sure you really need an agent; then remember, we are dealing with human nature here. Some agents act in highly unscrupulous ways, and some agents are wonderfully capable people who, even though they may have had a problem with one individual, may work out perfectly for you. A word of caution: The agent–author relationship is much like marriage. Before saying "I do," make certain you like your agent and they like you.

⑰

PUBLISHING AND NOT PUBLISHING

Bad book publishing contracts seem to propagate faster than spring rabbits, so this section is devoted to a few explanations and may hopefully clear up some misconceptions. The following are some definitions for the purpose of this chapter.

ROYALTY PUBLISHING

This is the easy one. A publisher takes your book and offers (you hope) an appealing advance and a royalty of somewhere between 8% and 15% on the retail price of the book. The publisher takes over the book—performing editing, typesetting, printing, distribution, and promotion. *Note:* You, the author, do your part by being available for book signings and assisting with as much of the promotion work as possible to help make your book a success. Never think for a moment that this endeavor does not require your involvement to be successful. Any good author knows that he or she must become involved in assisting with promotion. If you can give the publisher names of publications, bookstores, or any other outlets in your area that might be interested in carrying your book, the publisher will be more than happy to send publicity directly to these outlets. You should do your own "legwork" by contacting the outlets and offering to do book signings or assist in any other promotions. This action will make you beloved in the eyes of the publisher. *Never* assume that you are going to just go back to writing. You could, but this might mean your book will not be as successful as you could make it, thus making the book your first and last entry into the wonderful world of publishing.

SELF-PUBLISHING

You publish your book. You are responsible for either performing or contracting the editing, typesetting, printing, distribution, and promotion. This form of publishing used to be frowned upon by a major segment of the writing community, but with the conglomerates taking over publishing houses, it is becoming less suspect. Most self-publishers will tell you they love the control they have over their product and its promotion. Probably the most difficult part of being a self-publisher is distribution, which needs to be done nationally if the book is to be a success. There are several national distributors who will assist in distribution; the best of these, I feel, is Quality Books for library and school distribution or Baker and Taylor for general distribution. Should you decide upon this option, call National Writers Association, and they will furnish you with names and addresses.

Some self-publishers make mistakes during the process of publishing their first book. Here are a few things to keep in mind: First, saddle-stitch or comb bindings are less expensive than perfect binding, but they are also not accepted by most bookstores and libraries because the book cannot be displayed "spine out," which is the way most books are currently shelved. Second, no matter how adept you are at editing, it is nearly impossible to find all of your own mistakes, so find an editor or proofreader you trust before you self-publish your book.

Until recently, self-publishing a novel was totally out of the question. However, the best-selling novel *The Celestine Prophecy* was initially self-published and has become a major success. Successful self-published novels are not unheard of in today's market but do require major work on the part of the author to make them winners.

SELF-PUBLISHING WITH A BOOK PACKAGER

Currently, the National Writers Press offers the self-publishing author a variety of options. The press offers contact with a reasonably priced, excellent cover artist; a nominally priced editor; a typesetter; and an economical printer. Authors in this program can also opt for distribution through Ingram Book Company, the largest book wholesaler in the world.

PRINT ON DEMAND

Print on demand (POD) offers all the independence of self-publishing without the problem of storing 5,000 books in your basement or garage. With this feature, self-publishing authors are able to enter the world of publishing for a far lower initial investment and then go back to the POD printer for more copies as needed. To make POD a viable option, the author should consider printing up to 100 copies in the initial print run. Authors who consider POD should be aware that at the time of this writing, Barnes and Noble Bookstores nationally will not accept a POD book to place on their shelves due to the problem of not being able to return the book once it has been purchased.

CO-OP PUBLISHING

Currently being touted under a variety of names with similar results, in this option the author puts up part or all of the publication money. The publisher pays significantly higher royalties (usually in the 40% range). The author may assist with some of the promotion duties, but the publisher is responsible for all of the functions of editing, typesetting, printing, distribution, and promotion. The author has some, but not significant, control over the end product or the distribution.

The problems I see with this option are similar to those with vanity publishing. First, the author has little input concerning distribution. Most co-op publishers do not have a wide distribution network, and therefore the books simply do not see the light of a bookstore or library shelf. Also, many times the quality of the product produced by co-op publishers is substandard in cover quality, paper quality, editing, and other aspects, which may eventually lead to national distribution centers refusing to take the book.

VANITY PUBLISHING

You pay all of the production cost. If you want an edit, you'd better have it done. The publisher is responsible for typesetting and printing. Promotion is minimal. (Vanity publishers insist they do promote books, but the extent of those promotions is minimal.) Distribution is minimal. After much begging and pleading, you might end up with 5,000 books in your basement. I know of very few happy or successful authors who have chosen to go this route with their books. *Note*: How can an author recognize a vanity press? A tip-off for vanity and co-op publishers usually comes in their gushy letters that rave about how they *love* your book.

As long as you are knowledgeable about the problems involved with any one of these options, you can find happiness in the world of publishing. However, the uninitiated and uninformed end up not only in financial shambles but totally disillusioned.

SUMMARY

Several types of publishing exist; you can be happy with any of these types if you understand what you are getting into.

☞ EXERCISE

Spend some time considering the right type of publishing for you and why. Jot down notes, and go back to that local bookstore to determine who published the books like yours.

- Royalty publishing: A company takes your book and does all the work from beginning through distribution and marketing.
- Self-publishing: You publish your own book and take responsibility for all aspects of the production through marketing.
- Self-publishing with a book packager: This offers the author the ability to have the best of all royalty and self-publishing features.
- Print on demand: You are able to have your book printed for a lower cost and fewer copies.
- Co-op publishing: You furnish all or part of the production costs, and the company does the production through marketing.
- Vanity publishing: You pay all the production costs and must promote your own work if you wish it to be successful.

18

MARKETING AND SELLING YOUR WORK

Once you have an idea for an article, short story, poem, or novel, you face the greatest challenge of your career—selling your work. The work is not over with the finished piece; it is only beginning. Now the task of finding exactly the right niche for your writing begins.

MARKETING NONFICTION

If you are writing nonfiction, decide what magazine or book publisher is the best target for your work. In the case of articles, do not write the piece, but do gather enough information on your subject to be able to write the piece *quickly* if necessary. Then send query letters to the most likely prospects. Include a self-addressed stamped envelope for the editor's response and wait for a go-ahead. Most editors will not immediately say they will buy the piece. They will usually tell you to write the piece on speculation. Unless your writing is hideously bad or other circumstances beyond your control occur, the editor will generally purchase the piece. Note the word *quickly* in my above explanation of gathering information. Here's a quick "war story" about writing quickly.

I wrote a query letter regarding an unusual ghost story in a local mountain town. On Wednesday, April 27, I received a call from the editor of a publication requesting the story for his May issue. He insisted that I tell him how fast I could get the article to him. I finally told him I could get it to him by the following Monday. Because photos were involved, I called a local photographer to request the possibility of having him make several black-and-white prints for me and then rushed the negatives to him. Back home I roughed the article out from my collected research. The photos were ready by Friday morning, and I picked them up from the photographer on the way to the post office to mail the final package. If I had not completed my research, I couldn't have written the article and delivered it in a hurry. I wouldn't have made the sale. However, if the article had already been written, the slant might not have been appropriate for this publication, and I would have lost a sale because the material was not right for the editor. *Research first, query second, write last.*

Travel articles are the only exception to the articles rule. They can be written in advance and submitted to newspaper travel editors simultaneously as long as the papers are not within a 100-mile radius of each other. Novels, poetry, and short stories need to be complete before marketing begins.

MARKET GUIDES

For the purposes of this book, I am not listing specific markets. Markets that may be open at the time this book was written may be closed or nonexistent next week. So the best assistance this book can give is to tell you where to look for information.

A word of caution regarding marketing guides in general: Many times the information in a marketing guide is out of date before the guide is printed. Publishers become overstocked with certain material, editors change houses, or in some cases the publisher goes out of business. It is always advisable to obtain a current copy of the magazine you are interested in submitting to or to call the book publisher for a current list of editors.

A new and excellent source of marketing guides is the Internet. Many publications, including the Writer's Digest books, are now accessible online. Although these are not changed with any more frequency than the published versions, they are easy to research. The Internet also contains a plethora of information about publications. It is the best source for checking the website of a particular magazine to make sure the editor you are querying is still with that publisher.

Literary Market Place

The *Literary Market Place*, or *LMP*, is issued annually by the Reed Reference Group or R. R. Bowker Company. More recently it is also available for a fee online. Initially, the *LMP* listed names of editors in each book publishing house for certain genres and departments, thereby giving the writer assistance in directing a manuscript to the correct editor. In recent years, possibly because of the large movement of editors between houses, most publishers have deleted this information from their *LMP* listing, but most now list a 1-800 phone number, so a quick call to the house can give you the proper editor for your work. *Do not try to speak directly with the editor*. Most editors are extremely busy, and discussing your work with them can hurt rather than help your submission. Again, the *LMP* lists only book publishers and is not the best information for articles, short stories, or poetry. One final note: The *LMP* is an expensive book; I suggest you use the copy at your local library.

Writer's Market

Each year Writer's Digest Books (F & W Publications) releases a new volume of the *Writer's Market*. This market guide lists the names of publishers by specialties, editors, requirements, and, occasionally, payment scales. It is moving toward being available only online, so search there if you can not find it in your local bookstore. It lists markets for books, magazines, and screenplays, as well as a limited listing of poetry markets. This publication also lists a small number of agents. However, the comprehensive agents list is now contained in a special book, the *Guide to Literary Agents*. Poetry markets are also listed in a special publication, *Poet's Market*.

The Writer's Handbook

The Writer magazine also produces an annual publication called *The Writer's Handbook*. This book lists markets by specialty and subject matter. If a publication takes short stories, poetry, and articles, it is listed in each category—an extremely helpful feature for those writers working in several fields and with several articles or short stories to sell. The first part of this market guide also includes helpful articles written by successful writers in a variety of fields. This feature is useful to beginning writers. *Writer's Handbook* also includes a limited list of markets for plays and a short list of agents in addition to its listing of book and magazine publishers.

International Directory of Little Magazines and Small Presses

Published and updated yearly, the *International Directory of Little Magazines and Small Presses* contains listings for more than 5,000 smaller publishers. Many of these magazines and presses listed pay in copies, or less than 1 cent per word, but these are ideal for the beginning writer. Most of the magazines listed are not deluged with material, which means the beginning writer has an opportunity to find a market perhaps quicker than in the major publications. The second advantage is that these publications can still be used as a "clip" for your vita sheet, résumé, or query to a larger publication. Markets in the *International Directory* are not only listed in the back by area of interest, but the entire directory is listed in alphabetical order. Book publishers listed in this book are frequently those who do small print runs and are an excellent source if the writer is seeking a publisher for their poetry chapbook.

OTHER MARKETING AVENUES

Writer's groups, magazines, and organizations offer other means of marketing your work. Magazines like *The Writer* and *Writer's Digest* offer monthly columns that examine new and existing markets. Smaller publications, such as *Byline* magazine and *Authorship*, also have limited information on the latest publication releases. Larger libraries in your area may also have copies of the latest *Standard Rate and Data Service* guides. Although this guide is used primarily for obtaining advertising rates for publications, the front of the listings also includes new magazines that are being or will be published.

Writer's Groups

If you live near a large metropolitan area, you can probably locate some local writer's organizations. These groups will offer support with critiquing assistance of your writing from other members of the organization or, in many instances, networking. Occasionally, members of the group will know of other markets looking for new writers or, in some cases, may assist other members in writing for established markets they know might be appropriate to their work.

Online Writer's Groups

The modern writer may also want to take a look at the various writer's organizations and bulletin boards available online. The major computer bulletin board services all have a writer's bulletin board on their network. A word of caution to beginners: My advice would be to check into these areas a few times before dumping your hard work onto the bulletin board. Remember, it is very easy to criticize someone who isn't looking you in the eye. I've known a few writers who were devastated by online critics who treated their work like fresh carrion set before the starving vultures.

Writer's Organizations

National organizations offer a variety of services for writers. Poets and Writers, PEN International, The Authors Guild, National Writers Association, and American Society of Journalists and Authors are just a few of these many organizations. There are also organizations for specific interests, such as Mystery Writers of America, Western Writers of America, and Romance Writers of America. Your local library should have a listing of these groups. There is also a listing in the *LMP*, *The Writer's*

☞ **EXERCISE**

Use an available marketing book to find at least two possible markets for the
work you are currently producing.

Handbook, and the latest edition of *Writer's Market*. While most of
these organizations are open for membership only if you are a published
writer, a few accept and are willing to assist beginning writers.

The National Writers Association (NWA) is one of the few writers'
service organizations open to both beginning and professional writers.
NWA's services include complaint service—for writers having difficulty
in obtaining return of their manuscripts or payment for their work—
more than 100 research reports on everything from formatting manuscripts to selling screenplays, critiquing service, editing service, contract
review service, personal or telephone consultations on writing, and a
quarterly magazine. Membership is open to anyone with an interest in
writing. Regular memberships for nonpublished writers are $65; they're
$85 for professional members who have three published and paid
articles, short stories, or poems in a national or regional magazine or a
royalty-published book or royalty-produced play or screenplay or are
working in the capacity of a writer/journalist with their major income
derived from writing. Student memberships are accepted with a copy of
the student ID at $35 per year.

Most writers feel that membership in an organization keeps them in
contact with other writers in what can be a very solitary profession. The
support offered by other members and organizational staff gives writers
the help they need when they need it.

SUMMARY

Marketing guides, such as the current *Writer's Market*, *Writer's Handbook*, *International Directory*, or *LMP*, can be valuable sources for finding publishers for your writing. Other sources of marketing information
include critique groups, writers organizations, or marketing groups.

19

FINAL THOUGHTS

Some final words to writers everywhere, and some exciting news for depressed writers out there. According to the Book Industry Study Group statistics, sales of hardcover adult books are projected to increase 3.3%. The book industry published a total of 135,000 titles in 2001, and adult fiction titles increased 20%. What does all of this mean to those of us diligently laboring over our yellow pads, typewriters, or computers? It means that reading and writing are still alive and thriving in the 21st century.

CLASSES, SEMINARS, AND WORKSHOPS

If you live in or near a major city, you should be able to find seminars, classes, workshops, or conferences in your area. If financially possible for you, these opportunities to meet and work with other writers should be taken. All writers who have ever attended a class, workshop, or conference will tell you how they returned to their own writing revitalized and excited about their own projects. Frequently, speakers at workshops and conferences are authorities in their particular area of writing and are willing to pass on a wealth of knowledge to the attendees.

If you decide to take writing classes, *always* take classes from instructors who are selling writers themselves. English teachers and others who are instructors without this background are not able to provide the perspective on the market that a selling writer can. If you want help with spelling, punctuation, and grammar, take a class from an English teacher. If you want to learn how to write, take a class from a writer.

OTHER ASSISTANCE FOR BEGINNERS

Some writers will find it helpful to find a mentor. This should be a writer who is more advanced than the beginner and can tutor the beginner with problems. A published writer is preferable. I consider one of the greatest assets to my career to be the addition of a writing mentor, Pat Stadley. Pat, in a few short lessons, developed a struggling writer into a selling professional.

BEWARE OF SCAMS

Unfortunately, in a desire for publication, many writers fall prey to unscrupulous agents, publishers, or others running a quick scheme for writers. Most of them result in hours of heartbreak and thousands of dollars. Check with the Better Business Bureau (BBB) or the National Writers Association when considering an agent or publisher. BBB keeps on file complaints of and problems with companies. The National Writers Association maintains a file of any agency or company that has not dealt fairly with writers.

SUGGESTED READINGS

The following are some books to make you feel better about the fact that you have decided to undertake one of the most difficult professions, even if it is just a hobby or a very bad habit:

- John Gardner's *On Becoming a Novelist* (New York: Harper and Row, 1983)
- Anne Lamott's *Bird by Bird: Some Instructions on Writing and Life* (New York: Anchor Books, 1995)
- Steven Pressfield's *The War of Art: Break Through the Blocks and Win Your Inner Creative Battles* (New York: Warner Books, 2003)

SOME THOUGHTS FOR REALLY NO REASON OTHER THAN THE FACT THAT THEY MAY HELP ON A DEPRESSING WRITING DAY

1. When I was 13, my mother found a science fiction short story I had written and called it trash. That was followed by a rather ceremonious cremation of the work in the cookstove.
2. When I was 14, my English teacher, in front of the entire class, called my creative writing the most stupid thing she had ever seen.
3. My college English professor returned my composition accompanied by the comment, "You'll never be a writer."

Maturity took care of my mother, suicide took care of the eighth-grade English teacher, and a heart attack took care of the English professor. Sometimes I smile inside when I think that I have published more books than the three of them combined. Aside from that, I imagine my success is due to being semitalented, stupidly persistent, and certifiably insane. It is my deepest feeling that these three qualities are at the heart of every writer.

Semitalented

Hemingway couldn't spell, yet it didn't stop him from writing.

Stupidly Persistent

Steven Coonts's book *Flight of the Intruder* received 43 rejection slips before it was published, and that's low compared to some.

Certifiably Insane

Edgar Allen Poe, Sylvia Plath, Virginia Woolf, and a host of others. Need I say more?

What Characteristics Do You Need to Be a Writer?

Only one—desire. It takes what I prefer to call the "fire in the belly." Most prolific writers tell you they have never had "writer's block." Why? The answer is simple—they don't have time. Writer's block is a contrivance, a procrastinator's paradise, an excuse for not working. If you can't think of the next sentence in your short story, write something else. That is what I am doing at this very minute.

One parting thought: This book is meant to give beginning writers the basics. You should know the rules—before you break them.

APPENDIX A: SAMPLE SYNOPSIS OF *A YEAR OF HEARTS*

Stephanie, Janelle, and Ted have been friends since high school. At one point in time, Janelle and Ted were engaged to be married, but something happened after high school when the three parted to go their separate ways in life. Janelle and Ted broke their engagement, and "always the friend," Stephanie has never been able to discover what drove two people who were so much in love away from each other. Whenever Stephanie has met with either Ted or Janelle in the ensuing 30 years, both have displayed a continued interest and concern for the other.

When Ted arrives at Stephanie's home after a long hiatus in Canada, Stephanie tells him that Janelle is getting a divorce and will soon be free. Ted confesses his continued love for Janelle.

Stephanie arranges for Janelle to meet her in the northern Colorado town of Loveland. She doesn't tell Janelle that Ted has returned.

At the meeting, Ted tells Janelle he still loves her. Janelle confesses to still loving him but insists that her current involvement with her psychologist takes precedence over their 30-year love.

Ted returns to Canada to sell everything he owns before returning to Colorado to win Janelle's love again. Janelle continues to vacillate between Ted and her current involvement. Ted calls Stephanie at frequent intervals and involves her in aiding him with sending cards and letters to Janelle.

When Stephanie's husband is killed in an auto accident, Ted drops his plans in Canada and returns to the States for the funeral and to help Stephanie. He spends time with Janelle, and everything seems to be going well by the time he returns to Canada to complete his business there. Because Janelle is going through a messy divorce, Ted continues to enlist Stephanie's aid in communicating with Janelle.

Returning to the States, Ted has Stephanie help him find a house and he establishes his contacts for a job. During a depressed evening with Ted, and with Stephanie upset over various events, Ted and Stephanie have a sexual liaison. The next morning, both are ashamed and regretful. Ted vows to move immediately and Stephanie assures him it will never happen again.

Stephanie helps Ted set up housekeeping in a rented house. The two keep in telephone communication, while Stephanie tries to convince Janelle to come and live with Ted.

Ted invites Janelle to a romantic dinner. Both Ted and Janelle insist that Stephanie accompany them. Stephanie tries to bow out of the situation but is not successful.

Janelle finally agrees to come and live with Ted. Their relationship is bumpy and both continue to rely on Stephanie as their sounding board and confidant. Stephanie tries without success to back out of the relationship. Janelle meets with Stephanie at lunch and infers that problems in the relationship between Ted and herself are Stephanie's fault. She demands that Stephanie not contact Ted or her.

Stephanie begins to put her life back together. She finishes a writing project and her son graduates from college and gets married. She is attacked in her home, and her son calls Ted to help her.

Finally, Janelle and Ted have a big fight. Janelle tells Ted once more that she wants him out of her life. Janelle leaves to return to her friend, the psychologist.

Ted threatens suicide. Stephanie finds him drunk and spends an entire night making sure he doesn't carry out the threat. Then she tries to convince Janelle to give the relationship one more chance. Janelle refuses to see Ted and blames Stephanie for butting into her life and messing it up. In the morning, Stephanie confesses to Ted that she has always loved him. Confused, Ted quits his job, tells Stephanie good-bye, and returns to Canada to start his life over again.

Stephanie promises Ted she will call him in a month to settle the relationship. After deciding that she has nothing to lose and everything to gain, Stephanie leaves her sons in charge of her Denver property and follows Ted to Canada. She tells Ted of her lifelong feelings for him and asks him to give her a month. Ted agrees.

APPENDIX B:
SAMPLE FIRST PAGE OF A BOOK

Sandy Whelchel
1 Any Street
Anytown, USA
987-654-3210
Social security number upon request
anyname@e-mailaddress.com

Approx. 85,000 words
Reprint rights

THE REWARD

by

Sandy Whelchel

APPENDIX C:
SAMPLE FIRST PAGE
OF A SHORT STORY OR ARTICLE

Sandy Whelchel
1 Any Street
Anytown, USA
987-654-3210
Social security number upon request
anyname@e-mailaddress.com

Approx. 2000 words
Reprint rights

THE REWARD

by

Sandy Whelchel

APPENDIX D:
SAMPLE QUERY

Date
Editor's Name
Any Publisher
1234 5th Ave.
Anytown, USA

Dear Editor's Name:

Where does one get the basics of writing? Yes, there are hundreds of books available on writing, but few cover the very basics of how to begin writing. What to do first? Do you need a computer? These and many other facets of writing are covered in *The Beginning Writer's Writing Book* by Sandy Whelchel.

I have been teaching writing classes for more than 20 years, first in my home, and currently as the executive director of the National Writers Association. My classes involve a no-nonsense practical approach to writing to sell. *The Beginning Writer's Writing Book* covers the basics of writing in this same manner.

The attached vita sheet gives a brief history of my writing credits.

Thank you for taking the time to consider this proposal.

Sincerely,
Sandy Whelchel

APPENDIX E:
SAMPLE OUTLINE OF A BOOK

Writing for Beginners
by
Sandy Whelchel

INTRODUCTION
Reasons for another writing book.
CHAPTER 1—Getting Started
A Place to Be—reasons for a permanent place to write.
Stocking Your Place—necessary books and equipment before beginning to write.
The remaining portion of the chapter covers personality traits necessary to be a writer and the necessity for a regular commitment to writing.
CHAPTER 2—Ideas, Ideas, Ideas
This chapter focuses on:

1. Where to get ideas: other printed matter, visual media, watching people, daydreaming, overheard conversations, your own life, and other possibilities.

2. Ways to keep ideas handy for use in your writing: journals, note-books, and notecards.

CHAPTER 3—Where Are You Going?

The differences between fiction and nonfiction writing are discussed. *This outline should continue in this manner through each chapter of the book.*

APPENDIX F:
SAMPLE COVER LETTER

Date
Editor's Name
Any Publisher
1234 5th Ave.
Anytown, USA

Dear Editor:

Thank you for your interest in my novel/short story/article. Enclosed is the manuscript for your perusal.

I look forward to hearing from you.

Sincerely,
John Q. Author

APPENDIX G:
MAJOR CHARACTER PROFILE

BASICS

Full name _____

Nickname _____

Sex _____ Age _____

Nationality _____

Citizenship _____

Marital status _____

Spouse's name _____

Children _____

PHYSICAL APPEARANCE

Height _____ Weight _____ Build _____

Eye color _____ Eye expression _____

Hair color/length _____ Skin tone _____

General health _____

Physical characteristics _____

Style of dress _____

PERSONALITY TRAITS

Intelligence _____
Sensitivity _____
Outlook on life _____
Organization _____
Self-discipline _____
Punctuality and dependability _____
Personal integrity _____
Wit _____
Sense of humor _____
Self-esteem _____
Courage _____
Openness _____
Attitudes
   Self _____
   Friends _____
   Strangers _____
Personal morality
   Sexual _____
   Religious beliefs _____
Others _____

RESIDENCE (DESCRIBE OR USE PHOTOS IF NECESSARY)

Location _____
Lives with _____

BACKGROUND

Date of birth_____
Hometown _____
Parents _____
   Relationship with _____
   Relationship with _____

Siblings (how many, names, relationship with each) _____
In-laws _____
   Relationship with _____
   Relationship with _____
Significant childhood events relative to this story_____
Education (level achieved and significant information)_____
Major life events (chronologically) _____
Notable achievements _____

PERSONAL INFORMATION AND HABITS

Goals and aspirations _____
Secret wishes and desires _____
Talents _____
Main interests _____
Sports or hobbies _____
Food preference _____
Entertainment preference _____
Personal appearance _____
Dominant habits and traits _____
Other significant information _____

PRESENT SITUATION

If not the main character, relationship to main character _____
Feelings toward main character _____
Occupation _____
Salary _____
Financial situation _____
Major possessions _____

APPENDIX H:
MINOR CHARACTER PROFILE

Full name _____

Nickname _____

Sex_____ Age_____

Relationship to main character _____

Quality of relationship _____

Nationality or ethnic description _____

Marital status_____

Physical appearance _____

Outstanding feature _____

Outstanding trait _____

Occupation _____

Activities in common with character _____

Significance in the story _____

APPENDIX I:
SAMPLE VITA SHEET

Sandra (Sandy) Whelchel
1 Any Street
Anytown, USA
Phone: 987-654-3210

VITA

Graduated University of Northern Colorado. Postgraduate work: UCLA, California State Los Angeles, and Pepperdine College; attended workshops sponsored by National Writers Association and Southwest Writers; completed writing courses sponsored by University of Colorado, Denver Center, and Metropolitan State College, Denver.

Taught elementary grades for 6 years in Colorado and California. Worked as a stringer and columnist for the *Denver Post, Parker News Press*, and *The Express* newspapers.

Lecturer on writing and historical events in the Parker, CO, area. Writing teacher for Arapahoe Community College, Aurora Parks and Recreation, and National Writers Association.

Married with two grown children.

Presently executive director for the National Writers Association.

CREDITS

Magazines

Articles published in *Writer's Journal, Writer's World, Reunions, Peak to Peak, Ancestry Newsletter, Host, Jack and Jill, Child Life*, and *Children's Digest*. Short stories published in *Writer's Open Forum, Writer's World, California Horse Review*, and *Primary Treasure*. Former market columnist for *Gothic Journal*. Current editor of *Authorship*.

Newspapers

- *Parker Trail*, history columnist—1985 to present
- *Denver Post*—2 years
- *The Express*—2 years
- *Parker News Press*—4 years

Books

Nonfiction

- *Beginning Writer's Writing Book*—1996
- *A Guide to the U.S. Air Force Academy*—1990
- *Parker, Colorado: A Folk History*—1990
- *Your Air Force Academy*—1982

Coloring Books

- *A Day in Blue*—1984, 1986, 1990
- *A Day at the Cave*—1985
- *Prorodeo Hall of Champions*—1985
- *Pikes Peak Country*—1986, 1988, 1990
- *Mile High Denver*—1987

Fiction Books

- *Hide and Seek*—2006
- *Check and Mate*—2007

Booklet

- *The Register* (Parker Historic Sites)—1989

HONORS

Currently listed for writing accomplishments in *Marquis Who's Who of the World*, *Who's Who in the West*, *Who's Who of American Women*, and *Who's Who of Emerging Young Leaders*. Also listed in *Foremost Women of the Twentieth Century*, *International Authors and Writers Who's Who*, and *Who's Who in U.S. Writers, Editors and Poets*.

APPENDIX J:
SUGGESTED RELEASE
FORM FOR INTERVIEWS

In consideration for value received, receipt whereof acknowledged, I hereby give (name of interviewer) the absolute right and permission to copyright and/or publish or to have copyrighted or have published the information about me contained in the attached manuscript. I understand that the manuscript will undergo editing prior to any publication, and I consent to the use of the information in revised or edited form without first seeing the revised or edited manuscript.

I also hereby waive any right to inspect and/or approve not only the final edited-for-publication versions but also any advertising copy that may be used in connection therewith.

Date_____ Signature _____

Address _____

Witness _____

Note: The usual "value received" is 1 dollar or whatever monetary amount the author may wish to pay or is obligated to pay. However, the "remuneration" can consist solely of the gratification derived by the signee at seeing his or her name or story or photograph in print. It could, for example, include the copy of the manuscript attached to the agreement, or in the case of a photograph, it might be a copy print of that photograph.

INDEX

ABOUT THE AUTHOR

Sandy Whelchel is executive director of the National Writers Association and author of six nonfiction books, five coloring books, and two novels.